Bring Me My Bow

Bring Me My Bow

JOHN SEYMOUR

TURNSTONE BOOKS

Published by
Turnstone Books
37 Upper Addison Gardens
London W14 8AJ

©1977 John Seymour

Hardcover ISBN 0 85500 078 3
Paperback ISBN 0 85500 079 1

Typeset in 11/13 Plantin by
Saildean Limited, Kingston
Printed by Biddles Limited
Guildford

Contents

CHAPTER 1

Self-Sufficiency

I am a man who lives in the country, on a piece of land from which I try to produce my own food. Since I also write about this way of life, I am frequently told: 'You think you can solve all the ills of the world by persuading people to keep pigs!' As a matter of fact I do think some problems would be solved if more people kept these useful animals, but I have never tried to persuade anyone to keep a pig. I have merely tried to tell them how to do it if they want to.

However, having now written several practical books about self-sufficient living and having persuaded quite a few people to adopt this mode of life, I feel it is my duty to explain my own philosophy of self-sufficiency. This goes somewhat beyond the simple notion of a man trying to grow his own food and produce his own artefacts. It is not desirable, nor is it possible for every person in the world to live on his own land and grow all his own food. (Please note that, bowing to the inadequacies of the English language, I use he for he and she, man or mankind for the whole human race). I believe that the man who does take a piece of his own country and makes it more productive of food than it was before, without large-scale use of chemicals or machinery, is doing the most valuable thing he can. Nevertheless, there is more to it than this.

The word civilization is hard to define, though we all think we know what it means. The word barbarism is similarly hard to define, though we might say it is very nearly the opposite of civilization. A whole nation of self-sufficient peasants might be very far from barbarism, yet not be very near to civilization, at least not to high civilization. A nation of big-city dwellers may of course be very far from civilisation – very near to barbarism, in fact. But the nation of peasants needs more than just peasants to make it a civilized nation and so, liking civilization as I do, I do *not* advocate that everybody in the world should live my sort of life.

I can see the point of specialization. I know all about 'economy of scale'. I know about the cross-fertilizing effect of gathering people together in cities. (I use the word *city* here to mean something very much more civilized than the average vast twentieth century conurbation). I think cities are absolutely necessary for the nurturing of what I call civilization. Homer's Greece, where all men were peasants, might have been a lovely and innocent place; but I would have preferred to have lived in Plato's Greece, thank you. It had cities. They were just the right size, too.

No, I would *not* like to see every city person in the world flee his city, grab his piece of land and become 'self sufficient'. I would like to see a lot of them do this – but not all.

The extended meaning I wish to extract in this book from the words *self-sufficiency* is: an arrangement of society which allows every one of us to have more control over more of the things which affect us, which enables more of us to see the beginning, the middle, and the end, of more of the things that we do, and which enables more of us to know, personally, the people with whom we deal in trade, for whom we have to do things and who have to do things for us.

I think it is a fine thing if, when a man bites into a piece of bread, he can think to himself that he knows the name of the farmer who grew the wheat, the name of the miller who milled it, and the name of the baker who baked it. That is the kind of self sufficiency that I wish to discuss, and to advocate, in this book.

Ah! shout the orthodox economists. This man was boasting that he knows all about economy of scale – and yet here he is advocating a way of ordering things that completely ignores the value of such economy. What about the advantages of specialization? Has he never heard of the virtues of capital-intensive enterprise?

Way back in the dark ages of the science of economics, when William Cobbett used to call the practitioners of that science the *pheelosophers* (because most of them were Scottish for some reason), the economists themselves invented a lovely new law – the *law of diminishing returns*. This law applies to such things as economy of scale, specialization and capital intensive enterprise just as much as it applies to other things.

The law of diminishing returns says, for example, that if I put a hundredweight of fertilizer on an acre of land I will get a usefully increased return of money. In other words, for every pound I spend on fertilizer I will get perhaps ten pounds more for my crop, because it will be a bigger crop. But if, say, I put five hundredweight of fertilizer an acre on it I will get a lower return for every pound I spend. It may well be that I shall spend five pounds and get only sixteen pounds more for my crop. In other words I have multiplied by five my expenditure without multiplying by five the return I get from it. At this point it will still pay me. But from now on, every increase I make in expenditure on fertilizer brings a progressively lower return on my money, until I reach the absurd position when I am actually getting less return for more expenditure.

I describe thus (as far as I understand it) the law of diminishing returns because I think it a true law. I think the 'pheelosophers' whom Cobbett hated so much were correct when they dreamed it up, but I think the mistake they made was twofold: firstly they did not apply the law to enough subjects (the subject in my case being fertilizer) and secondly they applied it with only one aim – to make money.

I do not think that we shall understand what has gone wrong with our society until we begin to apply the law of diminishing returns to such subjects as: bigness (economy of scale that is), specialization, division of labour, capital-intensiveness, mechanization. And I also think that we should apply this law with other ends besides money in view: thus health, happiness, peace, harmony and even love, if that is not too embarrassing a word to be put into print. The economists have never applied it to any other end except money. Well, they can measure money.

I submit that we have carried the application of bigness, specialization and so on far beyond the points at which we have begun to experience a negative increase in returns in such ends as happiness, health, peace and love.

Just as an example: I grow nearly all my own food. If I had a neighbour willing to do it I might say 'You're better at keeping pigs than I am – I'm better at keeping cows. You supply me with bacon and I'll supply you with milk.' Now that would be division of labour, economy of scale, specialization. And I think that it would probably increase human health and happiness. It would make life easier for both me and my neighbour. It would be an arrangement that comes well below the point at which returns of happiness, for example, have reached the point of no increase. Suppose I go further and stop doing anything on my farm except keeping cows. Then I will have gone beyond the point at which returns and happiness have ceased to increase (oh yes – I may get more *money*. But my submission is that we have gone wrong because we do not consider other ends besides money). It will be boring to do nothing else except milk cows. The agricultural economists of the Ministry of Agriculture tell me that on my farm I should do nothing except keep dairy cows. But can you imagine anything more boring than milking a hundred dairy cows twice a day? The commercial dairy farmer never has time to look into the faces of his cows – he only has time to look at their arses, as he claps, endlessly, the milking machines on their udders. He's not interested in the faces – that's only where the cake goes in. Oh yes, the life of a big dairy farmer is definitely boring.

In other words, considering the above problem with specialization as a subject and happiness as an end I think that I would get a useful increase in happiness if I ceased keeping pigs, kept another cow and then exchanged milk for bacon with my neighbour; but I think I would get a negative return in end happiness if I increased specialization to the point at which I did nothing else except keep cows.

I believe that technological society has carried bigness, specialization, division of labour, capital intensiveness – and all the other panaceae of the *pheelosophers* far beyond the point at which diminishing returns have begun to become counter-productive, taking ends such as happiness, health, peace, etc. I believe that far too many workers in our society are bored and unhappy. I believe they hear the alarm clock with dread, they go to work in the morning with heavy hearts and are glad when it is time to go home again, and I think this is a tragedy, for work should be the happiest experience of all. It is, for some of us, and it should be for everyone. I believe that if people only have one life, then they are being cheated out of enjoying it. If they have an infinite number of lives, then they are being cheated out of enjoying this one. This is sad and wrong.

I would like to give one more example of this new interpretation of the law of diminishing returns. This time a more industrial one.

Let us return to our discussion of bread. The government, let us say, asks an economic adviser to advise how large the optimum-sized bakery for Great Britain should be. The economist takes for his subject 'size of bakery', for his end of course 'money'. He feeds his data into his computer and it comes up with the answer: the optimum size of bakery is one that would supply the whole of Wales. If it were smaller than this the loss of economy of scale, specialization, etc. would decrease the profits. If it were larger the cost of transport would cause returns to diminish to the point at which profits would, again, be less than they could be. Therefore, the economist would advise, there should be one bakery to supply the whole of Wales but no larger area. The West Midlands of England, for example, would have to have its own bakery.

Given the end the economist was asked to consider, he might well be right. Or he might come up with the answer: two bakeries to supply Wales - one in the North and one in the South. I have not got a computer so I can't work it out. But somewhere up the line there will come a point at which it will not pay to increase the size of our bakery.

Now, supposing the government asked the economist to make the same study but with several very different ends? This would, of course, turn the whole science of economics upside down. Just for fun, let us turn it upside down. For example, let us take happiness rather than money 'as the end to be achieved'. Well, money contributes to happiness, and in so far as the workers in a huge bakery are likely to be paid higher wages than workers in a small one this will cause us to favour a large one. But money is only one of the factors that favour happiness. Living in a small organic community is another. Working for a man you know - or even working for yourself - is another. Living in your own village and not having to emigrate to a vast city is another. Health is another: a man living in a village and working in a country bakery is likely to be healthier than a man working in a vast city bakery. So if we consider this subject of baking bread using size as our subject and happiness as our end we will probably get a different result. We will probably find that the point of diminishing returns occurs much lower on the scale of size than it did when the end we were considering was money.

Now we can repeat the same exercise with other ends besides happiness. Here are a few ends that we can try: freedom from road congestion, mental health, physical health, reduction of crime, increase in love of people one for another, fun, better educational chances for children and a multitude of other desirable things, including the baking of a good loaf of bread. Of course we would require a computer as big as the world to consider the vast number of factors that bear on the problem. Nothing is easier than working out such a simple sum using profit or money as the end. Any economist worth his salt could tell you after a few hours work that such and such a size of bakery is going to yield you the most profit on money invested, or profit per loaf baked. But what sort of a genius is required to plot the effects of having one huge bakery in a country the size of Wales on more intangible things? This could include the increase in the crime prevention bill (this goes up per capita in proportion to the size of cities), the mental health bill (the same), a lowering of the quality of education (almost always the bigger the city the worse the schools), increased congestion on the roads (through carrying wheat from the country to the mills, flour to the huge bakery, bread all over the country) and so on.

Of course no businessman is going to bother his head about such things as the ends I have listed above. If he is to survive as a businessman in the world we have today he is obliged to consider profit above all. He carefully works out the cost to himself of delivering his bread far and wide about the countryside, for example, and knows just where he is. If one of his baker's lorries (stuffed with 'Mother's Sunshine Super-loaves') happens to run over a child, that is sad but taken care of by insurance. If this huge fleet of lorries and delivery vans ruins the peace of the countryside and causes horrible conges-tion on the roads that is sad – but no concern of the businessman. If by ruining all the small country bakeries the big bakery forces people to emigrate into the city that is nothing to do with him either. If the quality of life in many villages is lowered by their losing what had been a major component of their industry – that, again, is not his affair.

We cannot *expect* the businessman to concern himself about

these things. He has been told the rules of the game and he sticks to them, and if he wins the prize (money) we cannot blame him.

Well, if we don't like the rules we must change them. I believe we can change the rules and force the businessman to behave in a manner more in accordance with our interests.

Now most of my fellow doomsters base their gloomy prognostications on the fact that the oil is going to run out. I cannot agree with this. I just do not care a fig whether the oil runs out or whether it doesn't. The current 'energy crisis' is only temporary anyway – the sheiks aren't going to withhold one barrel of oil from the West if it means foregoing one Cadillac or one fighter 'plane to have shot down by the Israelis. But I am indifferent to this question of the oil running out, and of whether or not atomic power can take over from it, because I do not believe that true civilization depends on that kind of power. The kind of civilization that I should like to live in – the kind that produced, for example, the poetry of Shakespeare, the music of Beethoven, the painting of Michaelangelo, the philosophy of Sophocles, the ribaldry of Rabelais, the prose of Fielding, the transcendentalism of the Upanishads – these civilizations existed when there was no power at all except wind power, water power, animal power and man power. Mozart never had a gramophone. Shakespeare never had a typewriter. Plato never had a computer. Michaelangelo never had acrylic paints. And yet these people produced very good results, and our present age – that has power beyond the wildest dreams of any age either past or future – can't touch 'em. No – my kind of civilization does not depend on oil or atomic power. In fact I think too much power makes civilization much more difficult to achieve.

Fear not – I am not going to start describing some sort of Utopia (or *Bluetopia* as a writer in *Punch* called it in a review of H. G. Wells *Men like Gods*, basing this name on the theory that Wells' Utopians, because naked, would have been cold). I know very well what society is like today, and I realize that we cannot *suddenly* turn it into something else. Most people have got to go on much as they are going on now, whether they live in a bed-sit in Notting Hill, a National Coal Board house in County Durham, a mansion in Wiltshire, or a self-sufficient holding in the Welsh mountains. A very few, as I have done, may break away from something and start something else. A small army of 'Hippies' roams the roads and sets up a new conventionalism. A few communities are set up here and there, some fail, others succeed. Such experiments are very valuable but they do not, and are not going to, change society as a whole.

If we want a more civilized, organic, decentralized, human-scale, satisfying, less boring, and less *dangerous* society nearly everyone must start working for it, quietly, slowly, patiently, and knowing what he is doing.

And if the great power shortage does come: if the sheiks suddenly take against Cadillacs, or the oil does get scarcer, and if men become unwilling to toil a thousand feet underground in abominable conditions, and if atomic power proves too impossibly dangerous to put up with, if 'they' – whoever 'they' are – don't find an 'answer', then we shall be forced into a more decentralized and self-sufficient society whether we like it or not. It is better, in that event, to like it, and to be prepared for it, and to move towards it not because we have got to, but because we want to.

To go of our own free will in fact.

CHAPTER 2

We Can't Stop Progress, Can We?

If 'progress' were inevitable (of course in a sense it is: time progresses whatever we do and we progress with it) but if progress towards a better life for more people were inevitable, and happening, then there would be no point in me writing this book. Even though the world is not absolutely perfect right now, all we would have to do is to sit back and wait for it to become perfect as the Victorians did. But if we have a feeling that the current progress is progress in the wrong direction then it is very important that we should work to see that we cease progressing in that direction and progress, instead, in another.

Country people in northern India clean their teeth with the chewed end of a piece of twig. It is a very pleasant manner of cleaning one's teeth and an efficient one, for these people have very good teeth. The bushes which provide the twigs are plentiful, they renew themselves as fast as the people break the twigs off them, and therefore it is a non-polluting and non-extractive way of cleaning one's teeth. In the West the tooth brush has been invented, and this is called 'progress'.

Now it is undoubtedly a progression of some sort or another, but the tooth brush is not necessarily better than the chewed twig. Perhaps it is more efficient at cleaning teeth (although we in the West have far more dental decay than Punjabi villagers) but perhaps it is worse in that it is yet another cause of over-centralization, remoteness, inhuman values, more dependance on things outside our control. Maybe this invention did harm in that it put more money in the pocket of somebody who already had too much money for his health and happiness. Perhaps it is boring to be a worker in a tooth brush factory, while it is pleasant to stroll out in the morning and pluck a twig. On the balance, though, I am prepared to accept that the invention of the tooth brush was a good thing.

Then somebody came along and invented the electric tooth brush. This again is progress, but I have no doubt in my mind whatever about what sort of progress this is: it is progress in the wrong direction. If we went back to the chewed twig that would be progress too – we would be progressing from electric tooth brush to a chewed twig. It is an incorrect interpretation of the word *progress* to assume that it always means progress from something simple to something more complicated. It is also incorrect to assume that it always means progress to something better.

'We can't stop progress!' is the parrot cry of the inane. Of course we can't stop progress, but we can decide in which direction we wish to progress. 'You can't turn the clock back!' is another such idiot's war cry. Well you can't answer that one at all, because it has absolutely no meaning. You can in fact turn the clock back – I turned mine back this morning, because it was too fast.

I am crazy about progress. I want us all to start progressing towards more decentralization – more self-sufficiency. So let me try and make clear what I mean by the self-sufficiency that I wish us all to progress towards.

A man who grows enough cabbages in his back garden makes himself self-sufficient in the matter of cabbages. A

17

village that has an adequate grinding mill in it is self-sufficient in the matter of grinding flour. A parish that has enough wheat farmers in it is self-sufficient in the matter of growing its own wheat. A town that has a brick works in it can be self-sufficient in the matter of bricks, although it may have to import coal from some other place to burn the bricks.

Now I know perfectly well that wheat grows better in, say, Canada that it does where I live, in Pembrokeshire in Wales. We have here a climate which is by no means perfect for the growing of wheat. And yet I still think it would be better for we people in Pembrokeshire if we were self-sufficient in the matter of wheat. This is where I, and other advocates of decentralization, differ completely from the orthodox economists. They say: allow the law of supply and demand to operate freely, and you will get the people of Canada doing what they do best – growing wheat, and the people of Pembrokeshire doing what they do best – producing milk. Then you will get better wheat, better milk, more of both, and cheaper.

Now to answer this apparently very strong argument I have to drag in the good old law of diminishing returns again. I don't believe it is a good idea for, say, the grocer in our village, to try to grow his own wheat in his little garden. I don't believe it is good for my neighbour George Hughes to grow his own wheat – his is a mountain farm and very unsuitable for it. I might be able to concede that it would be better for the farmers in my valley to concentrate on oats and barley and trade some of this for wheat with the people who live in West Pembrokeshire where wheat grows better. But I draw the line well short of Pembrokeshire not growing wheat at all (which it virtually doesn't – I am about the only person in my neck of the woods who does grow it) and getting all its wheat from England, most of it probably originally from Canada. Why? Because I think the law of diminishing returns has begun to operate here, if we consider specialization as our subject and happiness, or contentment, or the good life, as our end. Not *money* – if *profit*, or *money*, is taken as the end then then I think it would probably be better for us to get our wheat from Canada.

But you see we *can* grow wheat in Pembrokeshire, and Pembrokeshire used to be self-supporting in the matter of wheat. It is soft wheat and not hard, but that simply means that if we take to growing our own wheat again we have got to get used to a slightly different kind of bread. In fact in this particular case it is better bread, but that is irrelevant. If it were slightly worse – I'd still say we should grow our own wheat. For it would be better for us to eat slightly worse bread made from our own wheat than to import all our wheat from Canada.

I do not, though, recommend that we people in Pembroke-shire should grow our own avocado pears. I would put the point at which diminishing returns set in (*end happiness*) on the specialization scale, somewhere between growing our own wheat and trying to grow avocado pears. I think we should grow our own wheat, but either buy our avocado pears from the tropics, or else try to get along as best we can without them. I differ from the orthodox economists in placing the point at which diminishing returns set in on the specialization scale much lower than they do. But then I differ from them also in that I do not use *money* as the only *end* in consider-ing these matters. One of my daughters is learning Econo-mics at school. I asked her the other day what 'Economics' meant. She said 'It's about money.' Well I think it's not about money.

Now I must set to and give some very good reasons why I think it would be better for we farmers in Pembroke-shire to grow our own wheat instead of importing it from Canada.

Firstly, because it would make us more independent, prouder, men. It would make Pembrokeshire people proud to see fields of waving golden wheat in their county and to know that that was the wheat from which their daily bread was to be made. It would bring Pembrokeshire children in closer touch with reality if their teachers or parents could take them out and say: 'Look, children, that is a field of wheat. That's where our bread comes from. Rub an ear or two out in your hands and eat some. That's wheat.'

Secondly, to live in a countryside with a diversified agriculture and husbandry and industry is less *boring* than living in a world of monoculture. To do nothing but look after milk cows is *boring*. To live in a country where everybody does nothing but look after milk cows is *boring*. Further, by helping to force the Canadians into a less monoculturalist lifestyle we could help make life less boring for them too. It would be better for the Canadians if they lost some of their export market for wheat, and had to diversify their agriculture.

Thirdly, because monoculture, or the keeping of only one farm animal is bad husbandry and ultimately bad for the soil. We will deal more fully with this matter in our chapter on agriculture.

Fourthly, because growing our own wheat would (or could and should) revive the village mills. The benefits of this would be great and various. Employment would be provided where employment does most good – in the countryside (for in spite of all the supposed benefits of bigness – of *scale*, to use the current economists' gobbledegook – of specialization, division of labour and all the rest of it – we still have a very serious unemployment problem here). Further, it would give meaningful and enjoyable employment. It is more fun to work in a small mill where the boss is a friend – or an enemy (and if the latter well 'the world has many masters in it!' as an old man once told me, and if there were plenty of small mills you wouldn't have to stick to one). It is more interesting to know that you are grinding wheat that you saw growing in such and such a field, to supply flour to a baker with whom you were having a drink last night, to feed people whom you know. To work in a huge mill in some remote city, grinding wheat that comes from some part of the world that you will never see, in abominably noisy, dusty and inhuman surroundings, to feed people you don't really know exist is dull and impersonal. Ah, yes – the huge mill may be able to pay you more money. But it won't give you as much happiness or contentment.

Fifthly, self-sufficiency in the matter of wheat in Pembroke-shire would cut down drastically the amount of transport required. Ah! you may say, the man says he is worried about unemployment and here he is wishing to cut down trans-port, which gives employment. But besides being worried about unemployment I am also worried about misemploy-ment, and I think that the endless shuffling about of commod-ities from one side of the Earth to the other is foolish. I would prefer to see the army of people now employed shuffl-ing commodities about demobilized, so that they could drift into more useful and more pleasant occupations in city and countryside. The seat of a lorry driver's cab is the equal of the· businessman's desk as a royal road to the coronary and the gastric ulcer. Lorry drivers are a very unhealthy race.

In fact more self-sufficiency and less specialization would increase employment – not reduce it. A large number of small mills would employ more people to grind the flour of the nation than would the small handful of existing big port mills. As any economist will tell you – the big mills are more efficient in labour use than small ones. This efficiency will probably allow them to pay higher wages than could be paid by the small mills. But remember (may I term this Seymour's First Law?) we must never use the word efficiency without asking 'efficiency for what?' Efficiency for making more money for some fellow who's got a coronory already because he has too much money? Efficiency for paying men higher wages to live in a dreary housing estate in an unhealthy city and work at a dreary and monotonous job? Efficiency for what? Efficiency for making more people happier – now that is a kind of efficiency, too, and one I would like to see properly considered.

I would rather see the wages of mill workers drop, and mills become smaller and return to the villages where they used to operate.

My sixth reason for advocating the revival of the small mills is that small mills could not only be less polluting, they need not be polluting at all. There is more than enough water power, and wind power in this and probably every country, to drive all the grain milling that mankind requires. But such non-exhaustible sources of energy can only be applied to small scale enterprise. Wind and water cannot be used to drive the huge mills of Bristol and Hull, Chicago and London, Ontario. The latter are tied to using fuel which, whether fossil-fuel based or atomic, must always be polluting. To break the milling industry up into many small units again gives it the using of renewable and non-polluting sources of energy. These sources of energy are scattered, and can only be used by a scattered industry.

Seventhly, the revival of the village mill would inject some life and prosperity into the villages. For the miller and his merry men would spend some of the money they made in the village pub, at the village shop, at the carpenter's shop and the blacksmith's and the barber's and (eventually) at the under-taker's. Every small industry that can be started in a village injects some of the right sort of prosperity into the village. This is a far healthier kind of prosperity than that brought by holiday makers or city commuters, the large-scale high-technology industry of city capitalists, or by workers using the village as a dormitory and commuting miles to work in cars or buses.

Eighthly, reviving the small village mills would take some people out of the cities and find work for them in the countryside. This would be good for the cities. They are too big and they are overpopulated. To reduce their pop-ulation could only do them good. Start a mill here where I live, in Trefdraeth, Pembrokeshire, and you make life slightly better for the people who live in Avonmouth

You relieve, by a very little, the congestion there, the chronic housing shortage that every big city in the world suffers, no matter how many houses are built in it every year, the pollution, the danger of getting run over every time you cross the street, the run on the world's non-renewable sources of energy, the incidence of crime and the breakdown of mental health.

All right – you lose some Economy of Scale. It's worth it.

I would apply this principle of a fairly high degree of self-sufficiency to every industry, every activity of man, all up and down the scale of human units and communities. It is better for a man to grow his own cabbages in his back garden than to buy them. They will be fresher and less full of chemicals; a man will give himself healthy exercise growing them, he will amuse himself and give himself pride, he will take transport off the roads, and he will avoid putting money into the pockets of middlemen who already have more money than is good for their health or moral welfare.

But if the man doesn't want to grow his own cabbages, or can't, then it is better for him to buy them from a local market gardener, either direct, or through a small local shop, than to buy cabbages grown in some remote part of the country (somewhere where cabbages grow awfully well I admit) and trundled hundreds of miles over congested roads. And this *even if he has to pay a little bit more for the local cabbages*, and even if the cabbages aren't quite so perfect and unblemished. These tiny sacrifices are well worth making – if they help to lead to a happier and better society for every one of us.

Believe it or not nearly all the vegetables bought and sold in my county of Pembrokeshire are brought from the vegetable market, in the heart of London, two hundred and fifty miles away! There are two firms here, each of which has a huge lorry-load of vegetables from Covent Garden Market every day of the week. Can anything be more fatuous than that! Vegetables of all temperate sorts grow very well in Pembrokeshire. There is plenty of land here not being used at all. There are lots of people unemployed. And yet we get our vegetables from London, two hundred and fifty miles away. To such *degradation*, and it is nothing less, has the unrestrained search for Economy of Scale and Division of Labour and all the rest of it brought us. Of course a massive increase in the price of road transport will one day alter this ridiculous situation. But I suggest that we should not wait for this massive increase. We should do something about it now, before we are forced to.

As it happens, this example of vegetables is a little unfair for my argument. Vegetables grown locally and eaten fresh, preferably within a few hours of being picked, are in any case, infinitely better in both flavour and food value than vegetables grown – for example – in Bedfordshire, picked one day, trucked to Covent Garden Market the next, loaded on to a lorry and left overnight, driven two hundred and fifty miles, stacked in a depot, eventually collected by a retailer, taken to his shop and exposed for sale in Pembrokeshire. If you ask the retailer why he buys the Covent Garden vegetables he will reply: 'Because there is an assured supply of uniform articles throughout the year. The public buy on appearance, and these vegetables, grown by specialists, have an unblemished and above all uniform appearance.' Well it is time the public were educated into realizing that uniformity has got nothing to do with good flavour or good food value. A completely unblemished appearance all too often simply means that the plants have been sprayed with systemic insecticide or fungicide and the actual cells of the vegetables, which we eat, probably contain traces of toxic chemicals. Far better to take local fresh vegetables as they come, enjoying the fruits of the earth in their season. You will have the thrill of eating fresh green garden peas when they first arrive in June after many months of pealess existence, and celery, bought with the good earth still stuck to its roots, after the first frosts. The *pleasure* of eating vegetables is far greater if you can't get each vegetable all the year round but have to wait until its proper season.

If you agree with me about this little matter of vegetables you may say: 'Yes – but what can we do about it?' Well plenty. My purpose in writing this book is to show that there is plenty that we can do about such things. Firstly, *propaganda*. Help educate other people. Secondly *boycott*. Boycott the vegetables dragged hundreds of miles in the backs of lorries. Every time you go to the vegetable shop ask where what you want was grown. If hundreds of miles away say: 'No thanks – I'd prefer something fresh!' Say it in a loud voice, so the other customers can hear you! If there are fresh vegetables there, locally grown, buy some and congratulate the shopkeeper. If there aren't – go to a little trouble to find out where you can get local produce. If you can't – encourage a local man to grow some. Promise that you will support him. If you can't – well start growing vegetables yourself – to eat and for sale. Carry on a campaign, in other words, to put out of business the money-grubbers who are shuffling vegetables hundreds of miles about the countryside.

Of course there will always be trade. New York and London are not suddenly going to disappear, and neither of them has any coal mines. If they want coal they have got to import it from somewhere else. They will have to pay for this with manufactured goods, or other services. This will be trade. If we want avocado pears in Pembrokeshire then we must pay for them with some of the things that we can produce. That will be trade. I don't want to see no trade – I just want to see a lot less trade. Again I think that the Law of Diminishing Returns operates with trade as it does with so many other things. Some trade is good for us, but there comes a point in an increasing volume of trade when improvement begins to diminish, after this it stops altogether, and then the situation actually grows worse. I believe our society is miles past that point. It would be foolish for New Yorkers or Londoners to start digging for coal. If they want coal they should trade with somebody else. But I also think it foolish for Londoners or New Yorkers to buy Italian shoes. They should make their own shoes: it would do them good. The wool I clip from my sheep here in Wales goes to Italy to be made into blankets. You can buy Italian blankets in the shops here. I believe we should cease buying Italian blankets, cease sending them all our wool and learn to make our own blankets again. But I don't object to us selling them *some* of our wool and buying *wine* in exchange. For Wales is not a good grape growing country. That would be sensible trade.

In other words trade is good when there is a good reason for it. When it is simply generated by 'the blind workings of the market' then it is bad. We are not blind. We become less than men when we allow ourselves to be driven hither and thither by such forces.

Maybe the blankets we would make in Wales would not be quite as good as the ones they can make in Italy. So what! We should have to put up with slightly worse blankets, while we tried to become better at making them. The social benefits of reviving the wool industry in Wales would far outweigh any trifling inconvenience of having slightly less than perfect blankets for a while. The blind automatic workings of capitalism don't see it that way though. They are too finnickity. We must ignore them or adjust them – force them to serve our real interests. We are not blind. We are not automata. Capitalism was made for us, we were not made for capitalism.

Now it is no good making any recommendation about what we should do with this or that industry if the practical men of the world – the men who actually run the industries – cannot be convinced that our recommendations are sensible.

For example, going back to the industrial example we hit on by accident at the beginning of this chapter, flour milling, we might find this pattern of response. The manager of any of the huge mills in the United States or Europe, if he read what I have written on the subject, would say: the man is talking nonsense. He can know nothing about modern milling in the Western countries. He can have no conception of the vast *quantities* we have to deal with; the vast complexity of the trade, the enormous amounts imported, or shifted from place to place, the huge size of the market. To talk of reviving water mills is just romantic nonsense: the talk of a dreamer.

Now I do not blindly or exclusively advocate the revival of water mills. While we have oil by all means let us use it. While we have cheap electricity let us use that. If both these things become too expensive, there is certainly no reason why we should not start driving things by coal-fired steam engines again, or by wood-fired ones if we can grow enough wood. If water-power suits then let us use water-power. If wind suits us then let us use the wind. Use what is available, adaptable and preferably renewable.

I do not advocate the instant shutting down of the big city mills, or the instant cutting-off of wheat imported into the wheat-importing countries. I would merely like to see small village mills opening up all over the world in areas where wheat can reasonably be grown, to grind local wheat for local people. The huge port mills could go on grinding a-way as hard as ever. Maybe, in decades to come, they would find some of their trade falling away. So much the better. In any case, I fear Messrs Rank or Spiller need not worry yet a while.

Now to the question '*How* could we set about reviving the small mills again?'

Well certainly not by passing laws about it. I cannot think of any good that was ever done by passing laws. I think we must work as individuals. There *are* a few village mills about the country nowadays. Support them. Each one of us, as an individual, should support them. Even if the flour they grind is not *exactly* as your wife likes it – still buy it. Maybe your wife's taste can change. Maybe the miller can change. Even if you

27

have to go out of your way to get the flour of a small mill – go out of your way. Remember, when you spend money in your own countryside you stand a good chance of getting some of it back again. Be willing to pay a little more if necessary. You will get it back.

Take it one stage further. Working as individuals, help to create new small mills. Band together with other individuals – buy up an old mill building, renovate it, get it working. Pay a slight premium to local farmers to get them to bring you their grist to grind. Rely on the good will of other people who think like you to support you. If you become a small miller, make do with a lower standard of living than you are used to for a few years – it won't kill you. It might, in fact, do you good. Experiment and invent new milling machinery fitted for your type of 'intermediate technology'. For example, you don't necessarily have to use stone grinders. I grind very good flour with a slow-running plate mill driven from a tractor. Experiment. We don't have to be slaves to the past. We're not exhibits in a folk museum.

You new-style millers – don't neglect to use the most shameless propaganda. The big fellows do after all. You can too – not on the 'telly' like they do but in the street, in the pub, in peoples' houses. *Shame* them into buying your flour. Shame them into boycotting the village baker who still insists on buying Rank or Spiller's flour and go all out to support the baker who uses local flour. But see that the local flour is damned good!

It ought to be, for it need not be excessively refined, as is the flour used by the multiple bakers.

In all the above, for flour mill read practically *anything* else as well. Read textile mill, clothes factory, wood-working shop, saw-mill, foundry, light engineering shop, school, printing works, publishing house, paper mill, brickworks, tileworks, pottery, fish processing factory, slaughterhouse, smithy, tannery, shoe-making factory: the list is endless. Of course you can't start a motor-car factory in Little-Puddleton-in-the-Mud. For as long as we want motor-cars we've probably got to get them from Coventry or Detroit or somewhere like that. But the best marine diesels I ever saw in my life are made in the tiny, entirely 'non-industrial' town of Marstal, in Denmark. We can't do what we can't but we can do what we can.

CHAPTER 3

What is Wrong with What We've Got?

You may ask: 'What is so wrong with the world we've got? Why do you want to change it so radically?'

Apologists for the *status quo* say things like:

1. We are better off now than we have ever been before.
2. Life was all toil 'in those days'.
3. Modern men can't fit into medieval suits of armour, which shows that we are bigger than people of that period.
4. The civilizations of Plato, Beethoven and Shakespeare were only possible because of the existence of large numbers of slaves or helots.
5. In the past there was a very high child mortality rate and women used to die of puerperal fever. There was plague. There were wars. There was famine.
6. Life in 'the so-called good-old days' was nasty, brutish and short.

Now whatever happens I do not want to turn this book into an apologia for the past. My aim is to show where I think we have gone wrong and to suggest how we can work for a better future. We cannot hope to go sensibly into the future without considering, very carefully, what actually happened in the past. The North American entrepreneur who delivered himself of the statement: 'History is Bunk' showed himself a barbarian. I have no doubt that the world today is better in many ways than was the world of the past. It ought to be, oughtn't it? We have had longer to find things out. Let us hope that the world of the future will be better than the world of today. But, as an exercise, let us try to answer, or comment on, the list of statements that I have put into the mouth of my imaginary apologist for the present:

1. *We are better off now than we ever were.* Well, like the late lamented Professor Joad on the Brains Trust, I cannot answer this one without first saying: 'it all depends what you mean by better off.' For example, a poor man who is a smoker would think himself better off if a millionaire offered him an unlimited supply of cigarettes for the rest of his life. But it is questionable in what sense he would be better off. If this happened he would quite possibly die of lung cancer (which, I was told by somebody dying of it, is almost unbearably painful) long before he would otherwise have died, perhaps painlessly, of old age. Can he then be said to be better off? If you happen to *be* a millionaire, just make the experiment. Offer a poor man who is a smoker a life's supply of free cigarettes. I'll wager that he will accept your offer, and having accepted it he will think he is better off.

African tribesmen think they are better off when they can afford to buy sugar. But sugar doesn't make them healthier – it makes them unhealthier and therefore, in the end, unhappier. Happiness depends more than anything else on health. Englishmen think they are better off when they get richer. Very often, though, getting richer does not make them happier at all – it makes them unhappier. Anybody can think of a thousand other instances of people thinking they are better off when they are, in fact, worse off. It is only the very wise man who knows what is good for him.

2. *Life was all toil 'in those days'.* Well? Have you ever spent a

few months doing steady manual labour out of doors? If you have, then can you honestly say that, once you got over the initial shock of it, you did not feel better, eat better, sleep better, make love better and think better? Physical toil in the open air, at work one can see the sense of doing, is pleasant, delightful and very good for us.

To obtain an idea of what it was like to be a peasant in Europe in the Middle Ages we have only to go to countries in which social, industrial and agricultural development today is still at a medieval stage. When I first went to Ethiopia, in 1940, that country was still a perfect example of a feudal medieval state. In spite of the war the peasants were still carrying on their peaceful agricultural and pastoral pursuits and I could observe that life was *not* 'all toil'. I saw them harvesting their heavy crops of ancient bearded wheat, and working quite hard at it, but I also saw them sitting in the evenings, after their day's work, drinking large quantities of *tej*, or honey beer, talking, singing, dancing and enjoying themselves.

In a village called Barwasni, in the Punjab in Northern India, I once spent a very pleasant couple of months as the guest of a villager during the sugar cane harvesting season. I used to watch the men stroll out (yes I mean stroll) in the early morning and, in a couple of hours, cut enough cane for the day. They would cart it back in little bullock carts and then spend the rest of the day sitting on *charpoys* (string beds) smoking their hubble-bubbles, which were set about the cane mills and boiling pans. The little boys of the village would beg for a turn at squatting on the ground near the mill to feed the cane in (they had to duck their heads down so that the pole that the bullock was pulling could go over it!). Meanwhile the men took turns, aided by the women, at boiling the resultant juice over a fire fed by the spent cane. Out of every ten people round a mill perhaps three were working while the others were charpoy-sitting.

I was amazed there, as I had been in Ethiopia, at the leisurely pace at which country life went on. Because of twenty years of subjection to the propaganda of Oxfam and other fund-raising advertisements, most Western people think of India only as a land of starving people. Many people are on or near starvation level, especially in the huge cities and in very overpopulated parts of the country, but there certainly weren't any at Barwasni. In fact on my travels I never saw anybody there who was not extremely well fed, and that includes Harijans or 'untouchables'.

I don't personally recommend the excessively indolent manner of working of the sugar-boilers. I merely describe it to try to demonstrate that in a medieval-style economy life was not 'all toil'. You have only to look at the plethora of holy days on a calendar of medieval times (and these were of course holidays besides being holy) to realize that the peasant who was tied to the soil had plenty of free time. More, I would hazard, than a worker in a motor car factory has today. Suppose you took away the great weight of parasites that the peasant of those days had to support on his back! The lords and the ladies and barons and squires and kings and toadies and all the rest of them, so that the peasant got the benefit of all his labour. How would it have been then?

3. *Modern men cannot fit into medieval suits of armour.* I don't give a damn.

4. *Civilizations of the past were only possible because of slaves and helots.* Well so much the worse for the civilizations of the past. We must see that this state of affairs does not obtain in the civilizations of the future.

5. *In the past there was high child mortality; also plagues, famine and war.* Clearly it is better for us to limit our numbers by birth control than by high infant mortality, plague etc; statistically, though, it comes to the same thing in the end. If the lives of the people of old *were* short, well some of them managed to do quite a lot with the time they had got. Think of a dozen Elizabethan poets and dramatists, for example, and compare them with any dozen we have writing in English today. If our modern poets and dramatists live a thousand years

they won't come anywhere near their forebears, no matter how short the latters' lives might have been.

6. *Life in the old days was nasty, brutish and short.* Some years ago I was commissioned by the BBC to make a series of recorded sound programmes of the memories of very old country people. I recorded a total of forty-two people, all of whom remembered a way of life which was essentially pre-industrial. (Yes, I know when the Industrial Revolution is supposed to have come to England, but it was at first an urban phenomenon and these people lived in remote rural pockets. They nearly all remembered threshing with the flail, harvesting with the scythe and some even the sickle, and one old man could remember ploughing with oxen). Only *one* of them said that life in his younger days was worse than life is now! I know they may have seen life retrospectively through rose-coloured spectacles, but if it had been *so* bad surely more than one of them would have said so? But talking with these old people (after a couple of months of it I began to feel that I was *living in those times*) convinced me that the life they were recalling really had been more satisfying, for the ordinary country person, than it is, say, for a tractor driver on a big farm today.

True, a very few of them had had to scrape about for food at times. Actual excerpts from these recordings include: 'We used to be glad enough to catch a few old roach or perch out of the dyke to stew up to make a meal.' 'I mind my mother many a time coming back from the butchers with a pig's or sheep's head she'd paid a penny or two for. That'd make a good stew or a brawn that'd last us for days. People nowadays turn up their noses at such tack – but it never did us no harm. What don't kill 'll fatten my old Dad used to say.' 'My father'd catch an old hare with his lurcher dog. That'd be welcome – make a good meal in them days. Nowadays people'd sneer at it. Different times.'

But I didn't record *one* who remembered actually being hungry. Listen to Caleb Wright, windmiller, of Friston Mill,

Suffolk: 'I never knew anyone to be absolutely short of food. To be short – but not to be *hungry*. They used to take care. Food – there was plenty of it – that time o' day. Farm workers – they'd have for meat chiefly pork. 'Pig in the stye and pig in the pot' they used to say. They'd say of the pig 'we're only growing of it now.' They meant by that they were only letting it grow – they hadn't started fattening of it yet. They'd start to fatten six weeks before they killed it. A pig'd take two coomb of maize, a coomb of peas and a coomb of barley meal. They'd pay from four bob to ten bob for a weaner and boil up taters, swedes, carrots – anything they could get. They'd grow a lot of vegetables – people really *farmed* their allotments in them days. I never knew of anyone going hungry. We'd help one another you see. We were always exchanging vegetables, or meat, or anything. And after harvest the women and children would *glean* – they'd pick up sacks of corn, cut the ears off and thresh it with a frail and bring it to me and I'd grind it up for them.'

Mr Wright was talking of hard times. Listen to Arthur Lane, from Shropshire, still alive and known as Lane the Drum because he lives in a house which used to be the Drum and Monkey Inn. He is talking of life in 1904 when he was a fourteen-year old farm servant, 'living in' on a farm: 'We all lived in. Nine of us. Oh it was grand fun! Butcher used to bring us a lump of beef to last us a week, and it was boiled in the furnace, on the Sunday, and then a girl used to go on a Monday morning with a three-legged iron pot, ladle this pot full of broth out of the furnace and boil it – and we used to have to bread our own basins, ladle our own broth – and there was some of the beef on the table as well – *and* cheese – *good* living. And beer. Home brewed beer. Used to brew twice a year – March and October – didn't have any tea not the two years I was there. *Good* living! *Good* living!' So that's one old man's memory of the lowliest job there was in the 'Bad Old Days'.

I don't advocate that we should go back to the economy of those or any other days. But I really do think that we should

35

consider those times as they really were and not as the apologists for our present urban rat-race would wish us to see them.

One thing that was common to all these accounts by old country people was the squire. I formed the belief, listening to them, that the squire was like a huge weight that the rest of the villagers had to carry on their backs. Of course most of them said things like: 'Of course half the village worked for the squire. Half the girls was in service in the Big House, and if times was bad, and the farmers had to put men off, the squire'd give 'em a few bob to trim his lawns, sweep up leaves. You'd get a bob here or there beating or *brushing* as we used to call it – beating the pheasant coverts when the squire and the gentry were shooting. If the head keeper was pleased with the day there'd be a rabbit apiece for each brusher at the end of the day besides your half-crown. If he weren't pleased there'd be nothing. But we was never short of a rabbit – although my father did go to gaol for it once. But the village depended on the squire in them days – a good squire made all the difference. And so did a bad 'un, the wrong way round.'

But what they did not seem to realize was that every penny that the squire gave back to the villagers so magnamimously he had first *taken from them*. For the squire got every penny of his income from the rents for the farms and cottages on his estates. These rents were nothing but an enormous tax on the labour of every man and woman in the village. If all of this pilfered money had gone back into the village for services rendered it would have been bad but not so bad. But most of it was spent in high living in London or the Continent, or was invested in city industry. Even the few 'Improving Squires' of the eighteenth century, such as Coke of Norfolk, spent far more on their indulgences than they did on improving their estates. You have only to look at the vast collection of art treasures in Coke's great mansion at Holkham, collected by his uncle, to realize this. When Thomas Coke himself took over his fifty thousand acre estate he was extracting £2,000 annually from his tenants, and when he died he had bumped this up to £20,000. He had increased the productiveness of his tenants by having them taught improved methods of agriculture - but he squeezed much of it out of them again.

Supposing you could have taken an English village of 1900 and *removed the squire*; then, with no improvements in technology, so arranged village life that everybody had his fair share of the land, that all the men and women hitherto working for the squire now worked at productive labour for themselves and their fellow villagers, that nobody had to pay any rent (or that if they did that the money collected was put to good use for the benefit of the village), then wouldn't that village have been a happy and prosperous place?

Let us get back to the present, which is what we are really considering. I still have to demonstrate that technological society is not the best of all possible worlds.

In spite of a hundred and fifty years intensive development of labour saving devices we still have to spend most of our waking hours at work, so whether we enjoy our work or not is of paramount importance to us.

Some of us are very happy in our work. I am, but then I have opted out of industrial society. I conduct a strictly limited trade with it but am not of it. Many a man in it is no doubt contented too. But I believe the majority of men and women working in industrial enterprises today are not happy in their work. Now I know that you cannot measure happiness, and I know that you cannot even define what the word means. But we all know what it means. We all know that a girl packing chocolate caramels into cardboard boxes all day, or a man who spends his working hours loading crates on to lorries in an ugly draughty concrete loading bay, or a man driving a lorry hundreds of miles a day along fume-reeking roads - these people are not happy in their work. The girl packing chocolates may lose herself in the *musak*, and in dreams of pop stars, and thus not be actively unhappy, but she certainly cannot be said to be filling every minute of

her waking life with vibrant happiness. She is merely anaes-
thetising herself.

Of course the fact that you cannot measure this quality of
happiness, that you cannot even describe it, is what has driven
the orthodox economists so completely over to the money
standard. They have found themselves forced to measure
everything by money. It is the only standard they can get hold
of. Money they can count. For example they can compare very
precisely the wages of a bank clerk with those of a coal miner,
or with those of a self-supporting peasant. They have fallen
into the error of basing all their findings, their predictions,
their recommendations, on the money standard. By doing this
they have rendered their science, if science it is, completely
and utterly valueless.

I believe that the majority of people in industrial society are
not actively happy in their work.

What about at home?

Let's start with food. If you are used to good fresh country
food, as I am, you must find yourself absolutely *appalled* at the
stuff the city worker's wife dishes up to him when he goes
home. Take that pallid, pappy, tasteless muck she calls the
'wrapped sliced loaf'. It is a loaf of sorts, I suppose, but a loaf
of what? I have seen hungry pigs turn up their noses at it. It has
to have vitamins and calcium and what-not added to it, by law,
to turn it back into a food at all. The meat comes in little tiny
scrags because meat has become so expensive. Compare the
modern working man's 'joint' with Lane the Drum's great
boiler-full of beef in 'the furnace'! Our worker may find
himself served up with tinned beans and an egg that was laid
three weeks before, or with fish caught off Bear Island three
months before.

Most of what he eats will be tinned this and reconstituted
that. Unless he is very lucky everything he eats will have been
'processed' the way it is – not to make it better – but to make a
profit for the processer. The latter has bought the cheapest raw
material he can get, employed methods of the utmost scientific

sophistication to make it edible at all and to disguise the fact that it is not intrinsically very good, and gone to endless trouble to give it 'a long shelf life' (i.e. if the stuff doesn't get sold within a year or two it won't actually start to stink). He then puts a hundred times the energy he has put into all that into selling the stuff. The wrapper is designed with the utmost care and often far exceeds in value the stuff it contains. The *wrapper* - that's the thing the 'food processor' is really interested in.

Even more important is *advertising*. That's where the big money goes. That's why an ounce of proprietary wheat cereal costs fourteen times what an ounce of wheat costs. That's why every bit of food has cost far more than the total cost to the farmer, the haulage contractor, and the shop keeper.

Suffice to say that our working man does not get very good food. He almost certainly suffers from vitamin deficiency. He almost certainly has false teeth. He is likely to suffer, at one or another period of his life, from gastric or duodenal ulcer. Yet nearly every one of those forty-two very old country people I interviewed two decades ago had enjoyed almost perfect health during his life, often in spite of, or maybe because of, many years of very hard manual work, coupled with good, wholesome food.

Having had his supper, our man will do one of two things. He will either watch the television or he will go out to the pub. If he goes to the pub he will drink beer that, Heaven knows how, has been stripped of all virtue. I brew beer, from *malt* (barley that has been allowed to sprout) and *hops*, and you have the feeling when you drink it that it is doing you good. We won second prize this year with it at the local agricultural show. I am told that the huge brewing combines brew beer with exactly the same ingredients. How then do they get it to taste like fizzy, weak, coloured, slightly flavoured soda water? They do. At least if our working man goes to the pub he will meet other working men, will exercise his tongue and his ears, will tell and listen to jokes, will achieve a feeling of belonging with his fellow men.

If he sits at home and watches the television he will achieve nothing more than a dispeptic liver, sluggish heart, brain, lungs and bowels, round shoulders and varicose veins. He will learn nothing by watching television, because a person does not learn by sitting in a chair having knowledge poured over him. He can only learn by going out and grabbing knowledge. The search for knowledge must be ever active, never passive. Columbus didn't discover America by sitting at home watching television. Ah, says our imaginary apologist, your worker will never in his life have a chance of going to America but at least he may be shown a little of what America is like by watching television. Well he is unlikely to discover much that is worth while about America by sitting in an arm chair watching a glass screen. A young working man in Queen Elizabeth the First's time could actually *go* to America if he wanted to. He could sign on aboard the ship of an explorer, or a privateer. Nowadays the Hippies, who have opted right out of the industrial paradise, manage to get to India in droves. Anybody can get anywhere on this Earth if he really wants to, and always could.

Finally, our working man, sated with beer or telly, goes to bed. Whether he makes love with his wife or not we don't know (my guess is he's often not too tired but too *bored* to do so). We may assume that he sleeps. He is woken up, too soon, by the hideous screech of the alarm clock, dresses, swallows some soggy mess called 'breakfast food' (which must be good for him – hasn't he seen it advertised on 'telly' a thousand times?) and off he goes to that boring job again. On Saturday he goes and watches hired men play a childish game. On Sunday he sits and reads a newspaper filled with lurid accounts, court proceedings, mainly against people caught committing sexual offences. On Monday he goes back to work again.

For a fortnight a year he goes to the Costa Brava. He doesn't understand a word the natives are saying except when, in English, they ask him for money. He tries to find a pub as much as possible like the one he's left behind him, is miserable if he can't get fish and chips, and misses television while his wife yearns for Bingo. A hundred and seventy years of compulsory education have led to Bingo. If he decides not to go abroad he spends most of his fortnight slouched behind the steering wheel of a tin box on wheels breathing such of the exhaust fumes as manage to filter past his closed windows, shuffling along crowded roads in heavy traffic.

He hardly sees his wife before he rushes off to work in the morning, and very often, if he has children, he does not see them at all then. When he gets home his children will be too busy doing the enormous amount of homework that is thrust on them nowadays to be able to talk to him, and, anyway, when they have finished their homework they will take refuge in that universal anodyne – the telly. Our man may have a little time alone with his wife in the evening but, after all, what can they talk about? His boring day at office or factory or her boring day spent shopping for all that rubbish they have for food? Nowadays they are increasingly likely to discuss her boring day working in a factory or office too. For of course a hundred and fifty years of non-stop development of labour saving devices has led to more, not fewer, wives having to go out to work. Either way I'll warrant their conversation isn't going to be very scintillating. Of course they can talk about what they have seen on the telly.

Housing. The one thing that most of our post-war urban development has in common is that it is extremely boring. Not downright ugly, like the urban and suburban (yes and, alas, the rural) building of the 'between the wars' period but just *boring*.

Go to almost any housing estate in the British Isles and look at the houses. They are one big yawn. You won't be able to tell where you are by looking at them of course, because they are rarely in any way influenced by the regional architecture of the country they are in. In some stone-building areas like the Cotswolds the brick or breeze-block walls may have been rendered with cement or even, by some spendthrift councils, actually built of reconstituted stone – stone that has been pulverised and then used to make concrete blocks.

As far as the shape of the houses is concerned they will be identical from Land's End to John o' Groats, and they will be *boring*. They are forced to be badly proportioned anyway, because of the ridiculous and unnecessary building codes laid down by do-gooders in the last century. For example, the ceilings in the tiniest council house have to be at least eight-foot six high. The eight-foot-six high man has yet to be born, but the legislators of Victorian England, worried by the incidence of pulmonary tuberculosis, thought they could combat the latter by forcing people to have high ceilings. Now it was not the height of the ceiling that caused people to get T.B. but working in stuffy work places, bad nutrition, and insufficient fresh air. Yet we are still saddled with this foolish law. All sorts of good things – true size of rooms for example, which means floor area unless you happen to be a giraffe – have to be sacrificed for this quite unnecessary ceiling height. But all laws which interfere with peoples' liberty 'for their own good' fail to do what they are supposed to do and do something else instead.

The average council house looks enormous when seen from the outside, but go inside and you are staggered by the smallness of the rooms. This is minimal housing. Once you are in you are probably in for life. You are not allowed even to alter the shape of the fireplace if it doesn't suit you, for of course it's not your house. The Englishman's house is his castle? Ha! Nine times out of ten he doesn't even own it.

What does the inhabitant see when he looks out of the window? Why other council houses looking exactly like the one he is in. He has a tiny garden out the back of course but he is allowed to keep no livestock in it, no pets, there are often regulations about hanging out washing. I *love* to see washing hanging up near a house – it is a sign of industry, cleanliness of the right sort, self-respect, and life. I love to see livestock in a cottage garden, too. It is a sign of good husbandry, good management and a sound economy.

I lived for a week, illegally, in one of the shanty towns in the 'Western Areas' outside Johannesburg. This was supposed to be the most appalling slum in the world, and I can quite believe it was. While I was there I was taken by the host, who was a Zulu, to see one of the new 'estates' that was being built by the government to house the Africans. This 'estate' consisted of apparently endless rows of ugly little flat-roofed boxes, each row of boxes with an equally ugly row of outdoor W.C.s. behind it. The jakes were nearly as big as the 'houses'. These two sorts of building, and no other, marched row upon row for miles over the veld. The visual effect was somewhat the same as those enormous military grave yards on the fields of Flanders. My companion asked me what I thought of it. I said 'take me back to the shanty town. I'd rather live there!' He agreed with me. For in the shanty town you built your *own* house. You didn't wait for some government to build it for you. If the roof leaked that was your fault. If you wanted to alter your hovel you could. But here, you were like a rabbit on an enormous rabbit farm. The shanty town might destroy your physical health. This would destroy your very soul. It's name is Soweto.

I see little difference in our 'housing estates', except that the houses in ours are bigger and the jakes are inside them.

Now let us move to the wealthier suburbs of our town, to see in what a noble fashion Technological Man lives there.

Here the houses aren't called houses any more - they are called 'properties'. 'Look at that fine property over there!' we say. 'That's a fine property. I bet that property would fetch anything up to sixty thousand!' And we sit in our tin box on wheels and gaze at the 'property': at its tile-hung gable and at its pseudo-Tudor gable, and at the pebble-dash wall facing the road and at its Fletton brick wall facing the garden. At least we have to admit that the thing is idiosyncratic. And yet - although it has been designed by a man who calls himself an architect, and built by a man who calls himself a builder, and paid for by a man who calls himself a man of good taste, it is - as a rule - well quite *awful*.

If we knock at the door of one of these lush 'properties' do we find, inside, all happiness and contentment and the life beautiful?

No.

The owner of the 'property', if he is a businessman as he probably is, has that look about him that makes it so easy for a good cartoonist, such as Giles for example, to depict a businessman. If you analyse this cartoonist's image you will find that the component parts of it are all signs of bad health. The pot belly, the double chin, the puffy eyes, the look in the eyes which – if the cartoonist is a very good one – is apt to turn out to be a mixture of worry, tiredness, and greed.

If we can obtain the confidence of that businessman we will find out that above all he is *worried*. You name it, he is worried about it. He is worried about the people above him in the pecking order of his firm lest they peck him too hard – or are seen to be pecking him by other people. He is worried about the people below him lest they shoulder him out of the way and get above him. If he is the boss-man he is worried by other boss-men, about taxation, about 'labour getting out of hand', about the people he is employing not 'pulling their weight'.

When our businessman goes to his weekend house at the seaside and sits and gazes out over the wild and wistful ocean what does he think about? Why money. Does he *relax* when he is there? He does not. He sits and worries even harder because there he has got time to worry. He can even find time to worry here about his piles and his ulcer and the fact that the doctor warned him, last time, about his 'ticker' as he calls it.

What of his wife? Maybe we shall find that she at least can lead the life beautiful owing to the great sacrifices that her husband is making for her. Well Giles is very good at depicting her too, but if you won't take Giles' word for it go to the next meeting of your Conservative Women's Association, or else just look into one of those expensive cafés in a wealthy shopping street where fat women sit and eat revolting cream cakes. Do these women look vibrant, vital, healthy and contented? Look into their eyes and what do you see there? A look of nagging worry that they are not getting their absolute due from life. After all, the world should be spinning on its axis to please and delight them, the wives of very wealthy men. But does it? It does not. Is their husband a vibrant and passionate lover like a Spanish matador? He is not. Can they find a handsome young lover who will love them for themselves alone? They cannot. Are their servants sufficiently subservient? They are not. Are they worried about their teenage children? Well, yes, they are.

So we come to the children. In fact they probably aren't there; they have gone off with the Hippies to play guitar and smoke pot in a garret. If so, they have dealt the wickedest blow they could possibly have dealt to their doting mummy and rich daddy. They have thrown the only thing their parents have to offer them back in their faces. What of those who, knowing which side their bread is buttered, do cut their hair short and join the firm in due course. Well they become just like Daddy, and we have had a look at him.

Now I know well that this is an overdrawn picture, and not the whole picture. I know there are plenty of working men who do have fun, who till their allotments, race their pigeons, create strange objects out of fretwork, carry on all sorts of hobbies. I know there are plenty of men in the Welsh coal valleys who sing most beautifully in fine choirs, showing a far deeper and more sensitive appreciation of the music of Bach or Handel than many a professor of music. There are working men who read great books, who meditate, who love, who adore their children and actually spend some time with them, who are deeply concerned about their fellow men. But these are the working men who have come some way towards my goal of self-sufficiency! These people strongly reinforce my arguments. These are the people who demonstrate that the good life *can* be led: it is there to strive for provided you can to some extent opt out of Technological Heaven; only to that extent can you lead the good life.

There is an unconquerable spirit in Man, thank God. Even

the poor country devils who were flung into the great manufacturing cities a hundred years ago, to work fifteen hours a day in the hellish mills and at the blast furnaces, or down the dangerous mines, living in apalling slums, under-fed and under-paid, even they manage to hang on to their whippets and their greyhounds, their bull-terriors, their racing pigeons and their fighting cocks. No matter how awful the conditions forced on men by a bad society, a few will still still manage to find some chink or cranny in which to hide away and enjoy themselves. I'll bet in Stalin's Russia some people used to find real fun and enjoyment despite the secret police. In Orwell's 1984, if it comes (and it *will* come if we don't look out) some people will still manage to find such chinks and crannies. But this is no reason for not fighting hard to make our society the best it can be for *people*, not for commisars, or dictators, or politicians, or economists or over-nourished businessmen.

As you walk about the wealthier suburbs, I know you will find living and vital and vibrant people there too. And I think their numbers are increasing. Some may even be successful businessmen, or their wives or sons or daughters. Others are artists or professional men. You may go to parties in cities where not all the men have double chins and worried eyes and the women that dissatisfied look and those stupid hats. Again, though, these people only reinforce my arguments. For these are the people who, although they may know it not, are helping to build the self-sufficient society. They are working towards decentralism. They are questioning the values of a society which is dominated by Shell, I.C.I. and the Establishment. They may not be ready to build the new society yet but at least they are questioning the values of the old one.

Let us get back to our theme, which is to show that Technological Heaven is not the best of all possible societies.

Homo sapiens is not the only species. What effect does our present society have on the members of other species of animals and plants?

There has been such a lot of literature in the last few years from the Doomsday lobby that I really don't think we should waste time pulling it all out again here. I would merely urge the reader, if he has not already been convinced, to go to the nearest piece of countryside which is being 'farmed' in the latest technological manner and *look at it.* If you are a Londoner for example go and look at any bang-up-to-date farm in the grain belt of East Anglia. Count the number of species of animals and plants you can see there with the naked eye. Then take yourself off to a piece of country (if you can find one) which is being farmed in what you might call a 'primitive', pretty non-technological manner by peasant agriculturalists, and count the number of species of plant and animals that you see there.

Has our technological agri-businessman perhaps extinguished all these species of plant and animal, which cannot be turned directly into money, in order to give a more glorious life to the domestic animal? Here I must ask the reader to do something else for himself. Go to the nearest hen battery house (hen-Belsen), or large-scale technologically efficient pig-breeding unit (pig-Belsen), or calf-rearing unit (calf-Belsen) and hold your nose and go through the door. Then decide if you think the extermination of every species of plant and animal that cannot be turned directly into money by an agri-businessman is justified by the happiness and joy vouchsafed to the creatures that *can* be turned into money. Again, go to the nearest peasant country and compare the welfare of the animals kept by the peasants with the welfare of the animals you have just seen. Yes, I know, peasants in some countries may be cruel to their animals, kicking, beating and overloading them, but these are occasional and sporadic cruelties, not to be compared with the life-long deprivation and torture of the Belsen-house. The Belsen-house is the invention of the agri-businessman, not the peasant.

Of course, the wiping out of all species of plant or animal except for a few which can be turned into money for rich men, and the keeping of the few in conditions of revolting cruelty, might be justified if it leads to enormous happiness among the members of the species which perpetrated these enormities. I hope I have shown in the preceeding pages that this is not so. By torturing hens and pigs and calves we haven't succeeded in making ourselves so marvellously happy after all.

Of course there is Art. If our Technological Heaven is producing the most marvellous Art the world has ever seen, then perhaps we can forgive it a lot. The appreciation of Art is a subjective matter and I will refrain from discussing it here. For my part I will stick to Shakespeare Michaelangelo and Beethoven, thank you, and a few others like them, and I'll hang on and hope.

CHAPTER 4

The Horrible Disease of Gigantism

So much for the ills of our present society. What is the solution? My solution as you may well have guessed, is what I call self-sufficiency. Self-sufficiency is the opposite of sitting back and waiting for some 'them' to come and do everything for us. It means doing it ourselves. Self-sufficiency entails personal responsibility and implies a high degree of decentralization.

Unfortunately the power lovers of this world, and they of course are usually the power-holders of this world, are dead against this solution. The one thing the power-lover wants is control. He wants to control as many aspects of our lives as he can, and the sure way of doing this is by ever increasing centralization. He hates, above all things, to see power devolve into the hands of the people.

I do not say that all 'leaders' are evil. Many of them are most benign, but their very benignity makes them want power, for they think they know best, just as I think I know best and you, too, think you know best. They are in a position to act and we must comply with their actions.

Every human institution tends over the centuries, to get bigger and bigger. Whilst England today is physically no bigger than it was in William the Conqueror's time, it contains many times the number of people. The effective size of a country is regulated not by its land area but by its population. England in William's day was a small and manageable little estate. That despot was able to send a few monks and clerks all over it and put the entire population, more or less, into a book. Try doing that now – start, for example, in *Islington*. Further, in William's day there was far more devolution of power in the country than there is now. William was only nominally king. The actual ruling and governing was done by barons, in their little kingdoms of a few thousand people, and the only government that really concerned most people was the Court Leet or parish council.

In Queen Elizabeth's day the population was about five million, and that, in my submission, is as large as the population of any country should be. The population of Denmark is under that and Denmark is a most delightful country to be a citizen of. I spent a summer sailing around the creeks and inlets and islands of Denmark in a little boat. One thing that struck me was the absence of policemen. I didn't see one until I got to Copenhagen, after months of wandering, and I habitually used to leave my expensive cameras lying exposed to view in my open boat when I went ashore to the pub. I was also impressed with the honesty and politeness of the people, the absence of poverty, the absence of great wealth, the absence of unemployed, the existence of plenty of small but well-run and flourishing industries, the high standard of farming by peasant farmers, and the absence of desecration and spoliation of the countryside.

Critics may say that the picture I paint is nearly all negative – the absence of this and the absence of that. What about positive things – vitality, great art, creativity, high thinking, etc? Well in fact I was delighted by the art that I saw being created in Denmark. The appreciation of art is a subjective matter and I have no more right to pontificate about it than anybody else has. More great art was produced in Europe when the populations of its countries were around the five million mark than is produced today. How much of the literature, music, painting, sculpture or architecture produced in England during the last twenty-five years will survive three centuries?

I don't think that vast countries and huge masses of people create a suitable soil for art to grow in. The argument is irrelevant anyway. Produce a happy, carefree climate for people to live in and a minute proportion of them will either produce good art or else they won't. That is all there is about it. I know a few things that the huge 'nation states' and vast conurbations do produce. They produce war on a vast scale. They produce crime, mental and physical, ill-health, vulgar wealth and grinding poverty, prostitution, and a few other side-effects. But we have all got so used to these now that we hardly notice them any more.

I state that it is better to be a member of a small country than a big one. Any citizen of New Zealand can go and have a chat with his prime minister if he wants to. It is not very difficult for the citizen of Denmark to go and have an audience with his king. That is a good thing.

When we consider the government of the huge nation-states of today we have the impression of countries under intolerable strain. Consider the United States. Here is a constitution designed for a handful of tiny colonies strung out along the Atlantic seaboard now trying to cope with teeming millions of people. Result: crime and murder on a scale never before seen by mankind; widespread poverty and its invariable and disgusting concomittant great wealth; and what one can only call *government by gangster*. The only things that prevents this mish-mash from exploding and blowing us all up are constant colonial wars, which satisfy to some extent the almost insatiable craving for violence of the people. The only contented and peaceable people in the United States are the people who

51

have tried to opt out of normal society. The drop-outs may be the heralds of a new age.

England, thank God, is smaller, but it is still six times too big. It still suffers from the strains and stresses of huge countries. All its problems are caused by units which are too huge, too unwieldly, too unmanageable. All too often the attempted cure simply makes matters worse. The old county councils weren't working very well? So what does the central government do? Why knock several counties into one and make even bigger county councils. What will be the result of this? Bigger and more intractable problems, with the people trying to solve them even more remote from the people they are trying to solve them for.

The inventors of democracy – the people who started it all and really knew how to work it – were the inhabitants of the Greek city states. In those every citizen was his own representative. He could get up and express his views in the city council. The unit which is small enough for every man to make himself personally heard is the only unit that can possibly claim to be a democracy.

How can I make my voice heard in the 'Britain' of today?

There is an election on in five days time as I write this. We all have an effective choice between 'Labour' and 'Conservative'. Can anyone in the world believe that it matters a damn which one I vote for – or if I vote for neither? Fortunately, because I live in Wales, my choice is clear. I shall vote for Plaid Cymru, the devolutionist party. My men will not get in, but at least my tiny little voice will be heard, speaking out in favour of a country of humane size.

What is the cure for this beastly disease of gigantism? Break 'Great Britain' and the other huge nation-states up again. What do we want to be 'Great' for any more? I don't want to be 'Great' – I want to be wise, I want to be free, I want to be kind, I want to be happy. In what did our 'Greatness' consist anyway? In beating other people up and then saying to them: 'Look – we're the bosses of the Greatest Empire the World has ever seen!' Did this make the average Englishman wise, free, kind and happy? We took away the freedom of millions of other people to achieve whatever it was.

There were, and are, and I hope always will be great Englishmen. I am proud to be an Englishman as well as an East Anglian, although I have left both East Anglia and England to live in Wales. I am proud of the enormous contribution that English people have made to learning, to literature, to invention and all the rest of it. I am not a pacifist and I am proud of the dogged courage the ordinary working class Englishman, and the upper class ones too, showed for four years in the entrenched hell of the First World War – the same sort of courage that I saw myself in the jungles of Burma during the Second. But these men were not fighting to hang on to any 'Empire'. They were fighting for what they thought was right and for justice against tyranny. The average English working man at the start of Hitler's war might not have had much time for the Jews but by God he was not going to see them being herded into the gas chambers. This may sound like jingoism, like sabre-rattling, like Fascist-pig nonsense, but to me it is none of these things. It is generous admiration for people who behaved gallantly and generously.

I know that many people of other nations also behave gallantly and generously. How, though, can an English person fail to feel a surge of pride when he hears of the latest of the fantastically gallant rescues carried out by English lifeboatmen? Hardly a fishing village around our coasts but has had at least one 'lifeboat disaster', when a boat has overturned, or been smashed to pieces, and a whole little community been plunged at one blow into orphanhood and widowhood. Yet not once on such occasions has there not been an immediate press of volunteers to take the places of the lost men.

I have another sort of pride, more private, more intimate, more my own perhaps, and that is in being an East Anglian. Ah there could be a country! And to be a countryman of East Anglia would in no way lessen my pride at being an Englishman.

East Anglia *is* a nation, and as large as any nation ought to be. We East Anglians have our own dialect, our own peculiar intonation, our own wry dry humour, our own way of understanding each other. I remember when I was sitting on a streaming wet hillside in Burma with my black platoon (I was in an East African regiment) a white man came up bringing a party with some rations for us. I had never seen him before, but the moment he opened his mouth I knew he came from Suffolk. In an instant the war was forgotten, the monsoon ignored, and the Japs could go to hell. We were two East Anglians, talking in our own language about things that we knew about and loved and really understood. When he finally went away, several hours later, my m'Tende sergeant said: '*Mtu ule ndugu wako!* ' That man is your brother.

The world of men divides naturally into dialects and ethnic boundaries, and it was a terrible disaster when these were bulldozed into the huge, aggressive, 'nation-states' of today. When Garibaldi 'unified' Italy he did a great disservice to the people who lived there, and to the world. Can anybody really still believe that Frederick the 'Great' did us all good when he bulldozed the German dukedoms and principalities into one? Ten million widows and orphans might not believe it. Did Edward the First of England do an honourable deed when he ground the proud Welsh people into submission? 'Ruin sieze thee ruthless king!' and may confusion wait upon the banners of every power-mad aggrandiser.

Now I must brace myself for the counterblast from the people who always say, at this juncture of this particular argument: 'What we want is not more nations but fewer! We want to do away with nations altogether in fact. All men should unite in one nation, the nation of the world!'

I too would like to see people get together, sink their differences (or at least admit them) and acknowledge their common humanity.

But there will never be a 'nation of the world' until men are allowed to group themselves in their natural ethnic and linguistic groupings again. Surely it can be seen that one government for the whole world, one all-embracing nation would be about as far from real democracy as you could get? If a man cannot make his voice heard in England how the hell is he going to make it heard in the world? Among – what is the latest guess: four thousand million people – how much is the voice of one honest man going to count?

If there is ever a government of the world you can be sure of this: it will be a despotism, not only the biggest but also the most despotic.

It distresses me that Wales, my adopted country, can have no voice at the United Nations. If I still lived in East Anglia it would distress me that the East Anglian voice could not be heard at the United Nations. You may counter that Great Britain sends a representative to the United Nations, who speaks for both Wales and East Anglia. But when I actually hear the voice of the representative from Great Britain, do I hear anything of the voice of East Anglia or of Wales? I do not. All I hear is the flavourless, characterless accent of London officialese.

Great Britain is said to have 'entered Europe' recently. This seems simply to mean that the price of everything has leapt up while my neighbours don't seem to be getting any more for their milk. I feel absolutely no enthusiasm for having 'entered Europe'. The Welsh haven't entered Europe. They have been dragged into it by the scruff of their necks, by Westminster, or Whitehall. If Wales as a sovereign state made a decision to join Europe then we could indeed join Europe, and go into it with the Red Dragon of Cadwallader flying, our heads held high, and *Hen wlad fy nhadau* on our lips. That would be the way to go.

Certainly I would like 'One World'. But the greatest obstacle to brotherhood of man is the nation-state. We must sweep away the nation-state before we can have any world council or any real brotherhood of man. The only way you can sweep away these monstrosities is by first breaking them up. Break them up into the natural groupings of mankind. Let a Welsh voice, a Yorkshire voice, a Northumbrian voice be heard at a real Council of Europe! Then let the Council of Europe send its representatives to the Council of the World.

People who would like to be decentralists but can't quite make the jump say: If you do break up the nation-states into entities like East Anglia you will get government by small-minded provincials; government by the jobbing builder and the haberdasher. They will want to introduce hanging again. In Wales they will shut all the pubs on Sundays.

As to the latter, Heaven forfend! But surely it is better for the people of these natural areas to argue for themselves, and not to have rulings imposed on them from remote government above, no matter how 'advanced' and sophisticated the latter may be? If the majority of Welsh people vote for the pubs to be shut on Sunday again here in Pembrokeshire then I, as a resident, will have to go on doing what I do now, brewing my own beer, and meanwhile working hard to get a silly decision altered.

It's not enough just to break up the nation-states and form countries of a human size. We must form the latter with quite a new spirit in mind. There must be less government all along the line; fewer rules about pubs, or puppy-dogs, more trusting to the good sense of the individual.

We must restrain crime of course, but crime seems to dwindle as the size of nations dwindles. I am sure, from observations in the forty countries I have lived or travelled in so far, that crime varies in proportion to the size of the country. There is more crime *per head* in a large country than in a small one. A small country can afford to have fewer rules and regulations.

Before we start shivering and shaking at the idea of government by haberdasher in small states, let us have a look at the lot we've got now! Look at the governments of the world's biggest countries. Consider the quality of their politicians. The sort of people who want to govern are never the best sort of people. They are, after all, the people who want power, and such are never the wisest men. In a small country we can keep these servants of ours in order. If they don't do what we want them to do - look after the drains, keep the roads in repair, a few little things like that - then out with them! If they do do things we don't want them to do, such as interfering with our private lives, taxing us for silly and useless projects, rattling sabres at our neighbours - then out! They are our servants and we must be at liberty to fire them.

I remember being accosted by an 'officer' of the Forestry Commission when I was out walking in my forest one day and he ordered me out! I roared with laughter at him. My servant, whom I pay, dressed in a smart green suit paid for by my money, ordering me out of my own forest! Like hell.

If you are a member of a big nation-state can you really say that you admire and respect the people who 'govern' you? Do you really think they are serving your interests?

You may rightly point out how corrupt and unintelligent present local government often is. Why is it unintelligent and corrupt? Because none of we intelligent and uncorrupt people take any interest in it.

We know it doesn't deal with the issues which really matter to us, though it may affect our lives in all sorts of ways.

Suppose that Wales was a country of its own again, and that real power were devolved on the smaller regional councils so that the latter really could affect our lives; suppose we found democracy a real and living thing, not the complete sham it is now - then we honest and intelligent people would start taking a real and lively interest not only in our central government but also in our local governments. We would have to make it plain at the outset that we expected these servants of ours to leave us alone as much as possible. In the nation-states we suffer from far too much government.

What about war? comes the inevitable question from the apologists of the vast state. I'd a darn sight rather be in the middle of a war between East Anglia and Mercia than in the one I was in - between 'Great Britain' and the Japanese Empire. But I don't think there would be many such wars. I feel mankind has advanced beyond the need for wars like that. The only wars that could happen now are wars between the great 'conurbation' countries (to move an ugly word from one ugly meaning to another). Russia and China are very likely to go to war, and if they do they may well destroy the rest of us. Break those two molochs up and Kazakh and Sinkian are very unlikely to go to war. If they do, they will not have the power to harm the rest of us much. Why are they unlikely to? Because their neighbours, and world opinion, will make it difficult for them. After all, if Kazakh and Sinkian were sovereign states they would each have a representative in the Council of Asia, wouldn't they? They could argue their silly little boundary disputes out there.

Well, say the apologists of the *status quo*, that would be all right if the whole world decentralised at once. But if East Anglia, for example, did break away from Great Britain, how could she defend herself? She would be invaded at once.

Would she really? What good could the Russians or the Poles, for example, hope to gain from invading East Anglia that would outweigh the enormous harm they would suffer by thus antagonising the whole of world opinion? Why doesn't Russia invade Sweden now or England invade Eire, or Germany invade little Switzerland? Switzerland is a tiny country right in the cockpit of Europe and she's forgotten what it's like to have a war.

I have to admit that Demmark is an example of a small country that did not escape war by being small, but Russia didn't escape it by being big and she suffered far worse damage than Denmark did.

Of course if Great Britain broke up into, say, the old Heptarchy countries of Anglo-Saxon England, plus Scotland, Wales, Cornwall and the Isle of Man, the inhabitants of the British Isles need not thereby be rendered defenceless.

If you are not a pacifist consider for a moment one really democratic, solely defensive, very cheap and certainly very effective form of defence. Enlist every willing adult in the country into a Defence Force, somewhat on the lines of the Boer commandos that gave the English such a run-around in the South African War. Give everyone the most effective personal weapon of the time, make everyone engage in some training in his own locality once a year or so, and make everyone subject to call-up by his own local platoon commander on an outbreak of war.

When I lived in South West Africa before the war I received a notice that, as I was automatically a member of my local commando, I would be expected to present myself at the farm of my *veld cornet* with a horse, rifle, two hundred rounds of ammunition and food for a week, if required. I thought then what a cheap, simple, effective, and utterly democratic method of defence this was. The *veld cornet* had been elected by the members of his troop. The whole male population of the country was mobilised. No warlord in the world has ever been able to field an army of that size!

How could a rabble armed only with personal weapons defend itself against modern tanks and aeroplanes? If the wars of recent years have taught us anything it is that a patriotic peasantry can defend itself successfully, with the most meagre of armaments, against the greatest weight of sophisticated weaponry that a huge nation can throw. Look what happened to American arms in Vietnam. A greater weight of bombs was dropped on the nation of peasants than had been dropped before in the whole history of mankind; a huge modern army, airforce and navy were deployed, armed with the most sophisticated weaponry the world has ever seen. After a decade of effort, all this could not beat a 'rabble' of peasants armed with comparatively unsophisticated personal weapons. The United States and the world learnt that you cannot successfully conquer a determined peasant country any more.

Suppose that the people of a tiny country, even smaller than Switzerland, said to a powerful and aggressive neighbour: 'Right. We have no standing army, no navy, no air force. By doing without these things we are able to live much better than you do because we do not have that awful and perfectly wasteful expense. But if you invade our soil you will find every single person strong enough to carry a rifle up against you. Wherever you go in our country you will be shot at. You will find automatic rifles behind every hedge and rock, bazookas in every ditch, mines and booby traps in every road and house; every building in every town and city will be a fortress, every farmhouse and cottage in the country you will have individually to destroy before you can be sure you will not be shot at from it. What will you gain if you *do* conquer us? You have nothing to fear from us if you keep off our soil. We have no capacity for offensive action. We cannot invade you, or any of your friends. We are incapapable of invading anybody. But if you invade *us* it will cost you the good opinion of the whole world, a great many lives, great material loss, you may be bogged down in a bloody and expensive war that may last for generations, you may be driven out, or you may eventually 'conquer' us but if you do you will have absolutely nothing worth having conquered.'

Break up the nation-states and there will be very little war. Eire is not going to attack anybody. Wales would never attack anybody if she were given her independence. Can you imagine Arkansas suddenly attacking Oklahoma?

What an impossible idea, a lot of people will say. Such things may be theoretically desirable, but they are just not practicable. Break up the Dinosaurs said the little scuttling mammals of the Eocene and where are the Dinosaurs now?

There are ways in which every woman or man, acting as an individual, can work to break up the nation-state monsters that threaten to devour us all, and then work to build true nations in their place. I have seen the feeblest of little creatures, the soft-bodied white ant, bring down a mighty building.

CHAPTER 5

No Man Ever Made the Land

Except of course the Dutch, who've made bits of land here and there from time to time. If a man does make land out of the sea, then he should be entitled to that bit of land, and his assigns for ever.

Apart from this negligible factor no man ever made the land, and therefore no man is entitled to an inch more than his fair share of the Earth's surface. If ten men were cast up on a deserted island the only fair thing for them to do would be to divide the island up into ten parts of equal value (not equal area), and cast lots for them, so that each man had his rightful part. The *right* thing then for each man would be to govern his part of the island as a benevolent husbandman, making sure first that he and his family got enough to eat and adequate clothing and shelter, and secondly that the other forms of life on his land, or that he introduced to the land, should be well and fairly treated, no species being allowed to get too numerous or out of hand and every species contributing to the well-being of the whole community.

What has in fact happened to the land of the Earth? It has been grabbed. It has been grabbed by a few ruthless and relentless men who hold on to it, in the final resort by force,

61

and who thus do the rest of mankind out of their birthright.

The classical economists stated that three essentials are needed for all human industry: land, labour and capital. The more perceptive ones then discovered that capital was simply the accumulated product of labour acting on land. Capital is labour that has acted on land and been saved up. Labour can operate without capital but it can *never* operate without land.

You cannot even breathe without land. Even if you breathe in a boat, that boat was made on the land with the products of the land. The farmer must have land, as anyone can see, but so must the fisherman, miner, miser, the book writer, bookseller and book-maker. When I write this book I am savagely taxed because somebody has seized the land on which the trees were grown to produce the paper that my book is printed on. Therefore every copy of this book sold has to pay its tax to that landlord before it pays a penny to me. Even such books as are never sold still have to pay that tax to that landlord. The publisher, the binder, the printer, the bookseller – each one has to pay a tax to not one landlord but to many every step along the way. Therefore you, if you have bought this book, you have had to pay a far higher price for it than the price that would amply reward the labour and capital that has gone into making it.

The landlord is, ultimately, a man with a gun. He says to the rest of us: 'You cannot live without access to land. I hold the land. I will allow you to use a little of it if you pay me half of what you grow – half of what you make. If you try to seize your fair share of the Earth's surface I will call the police, and ultimately the army, and they will restrain you if necessary by killing you.'

The landlord, for exacting this enormous tax from the rest of us, gives absolutely nothing in return. He didn't make that land. If you trace back the title of a piece of land far enough you ultimately come to force. A tramp went to sleep in a field. The landlord came along and woke him up and told him he was trespassing. 'How did you come by the field?' asked the tramp. 'It was handed down to me by my ancestors,' said the squire. 'How did they come by it?' asked the tramp. 'They fought for it,' said the squire. 'Well I'll fight you for it!' said the tramp, taking his coat off.

This utter unfairness in the division of the ownership of the Earth's surface might not matter so much if it did not lead to such inefficiency – *real* inefficiency for making people happier. It is bad for men and bad for the land.

The first economist to recognize the stultifying effect of the preemption of land on every activity of Man was the nineteenth century American philosopher, Henry George. In his great book *Progress and Poverty* he inquired why, although mankind had made enormous strides in technical achievement, inventions which allowed one man in some cases to do the work of a hundred, or one man to produce a hundred times as much as a man could produce before, we *still* had appalling poverty in the world. The conclusion he came to was that whatever the improvement in technique, or in the productivity of man, the *landlord* is always there, even though he is often quite invisible, to hold out his hand and say 'Give me!' The fruits of the improvement go to him. And you have only to inquire into the rent of a square foot of land in the City of London, or in Manhattan, to see that this is so. Every time there is an improvement in productivity, up go ground rents to absorb the increased profit. If you trace the history of any industrial enterprise you can prove this very easily for yourself. When a woollen mill, as an example, was driven by water-power, the mill owner might have had to pay twenty pounds a year rent for the land on which it stood. An improvement in spinning or weaving machinery – and up shot the rent to a hundred pounds a year. In came steam power – more looms – and we find the rent at a thousand pounds a year. Electric power – more sophistication – and the rent at ten thousand pounds a year. Each improvement may bring a little more prosperity to the actual people who work the mill, but nothing like the prosperity they would have from their increased productivity if it were not for the vicious upward curve of rent.

After all, it is the *landlord* who is in the strong bargaining position. Where he is not curbed by rent-restriction laws (and these never operate as they should) he is in a position to say to his tenant: 'Give me or get out! If you don't pay my price there are a hundred other would-be tenants waiting outside.' And what is his price? Why as much, to a penny, as he knows the tenant can pay without actually going bankrupt.

Then the tenants should buy his piece of land, you may say. Right, he should, and if he possibly can he does – but when he does, such is the huge price that the landlord can exact for it that the tenant probably has to go into indebtedness for the rest of his life. He merely exchanges the rent to a landlord for interest payments to a money-lender such as a bank. But whether the tenant buys or goes on renting there is one man who is going to benefit, and that is the landlord. He'll either get it in dribs and drabs or he'll get it in one great lump, and if he does the latter then he'll use the money to grab more land – to perpetuate the evil that he does in his life.

Now it may sound from this that I am against landlords. I am not. I like them so much that I'd like to see *far more of them!* I'd like to see millions of them – not just thousands as there are now. When a man owns somewhere around his fair share of his own country – whether it's a square foot of a factory floor in Birmingham, two acres of black fen in Lincolnshire, five acres of heavy loam in Suffolk, twenty acres of valley land in Wales or a hundred acres of good hill grazing – *then* he owns about what he should. He owns what he needs, what is fair and what he can really look after.

Of course nobody can really 'own' the land, any more than he can 'own' the sky above it. But for the sake of expediency – indeed of survival – somebody has got to control the land so far as human affairs may go. Outside of my window now I can see a robin. He thinks he owns a part of what I call my garden. And from the robin's point of view he does. Other robins recognize his ownership and do not challenge it. The robin world would break up and robins become extinct if this respect for territory were to break down. But the slug out there that is no doubt crawling towards my cabbages thinks he owns that part of the garden too. And he does, in slug-law. If I want any cabbages I shall have to show him that he doesn't in mine.

But somehow we humans have to allot control of the surface of the Earth. Somebody has got to control every productive inch of it. It is obvious that if it were just thrown open for the use of everybody, as the Diggers and others would have it, then no crop would ever get planted – no improvement ever be done. A man must be given security to know that what he plants he will be allowed to reap, and when he drains a marsh he shall be allowed the use of it. Otherwise no marsh will ever get drained.

What are the alternative means of ensuring that land is properly and fairly controlled? The socialist-urban view is that land should benefit nobody. The urban man cannot see, anyway, that anybody would ever want to own land, and he feels that rural land should simply be looked upon as a factory floor to produce food for him, the urban man. I am talking now of the minority of urban men who know that food is produced on the land, and not just found ready processed and packed on the supermarket shelves. Such a man would like to nationalize the land. It should belong to 'the nation' and be farmed by 'technicians'.

My own view about this industrial-urban solution is that it is about the worst that could be found. Farming is not a job for 'technicians' any more than surgery is a job for butchers. I knew the country in Tanganyika (now Tanzania) where the great Ground Nut Scheme took place. If anyone has forgotten, this was an enormous scheme – on such a scale that it, like Concorde, went a long way towards bankrupting Great Britain. The aim was to clear hundreds of thousands of acres of bush in southern Tanganyika and grow groundnuts on the land. Now contrary to the press reports after the scheme failed, this land is excellent for growing groundnuts; the untutored African peasant could grow groundnuts there, can grow groundnuts there now and does. But the 'technicians' sent out by the government at such enormous expense, and with such a plethora of machinery, chemicals, and equipment of all kinds – they couldn't grow groundnuts. Why not? Because farming is a job for the farmer, who loves the land, and loves it because it is his own. It is for the man with a feeling and instinct for the land as well as, or even without, technical training, and for the man who is willing to work all the time that is necessary and not just go by the clock.

Wherever and whenever nationalized agriculture has been tried in this world it has failed in the first two tests that could be applied to it: it has failed to make a profit and it has failed to be productive. It is well known now how close the U.S.S.R. came to total disaster by a blanket policy of land nationalization, and it was only by allowing farming by groups, with the groups themselves benefitting from good production, that total starvation was averted. Even now, production per acre in Russia is pitiful, in spite of that technicians' cure-all – huge applications of nitrogenous fertilizer. The Russians would starve without American wheat.

The Chinese, by all acounts, have never fallen into the trap of huge scale government-run farming. In that country the unit of production is still basically the peasant – the peasant who has husbanded his land so well that the best land of China supports, and has supported for at least five thousand years, *five human beings per acre*. (In 'the free West' we now require two and a half acres of good agricultural land to support each person).

Community farming can work, and has been shown to work in many areas and periods. Consider for example the modern *kibbutzim* in Israel, or community farms run by various fundamentalist religious groups in North America, or the Cistercian communities in the middle ages. Individual farming can and does work. But nationalized farming has never, to my knowledge, worked anywhere or at any period in history.

The next urban solution then is: nationalise the land and

then let it out to farmers to farm as tenants. What on Earth is to be gained by that? The existing tenant farmer would merely find himself paying rent to another landlord and an even more remote one than the one he was lumbered with before. Knowing the tendency of all government enterprises to proliferate officials, you can be sure that this new landlord would soon be charging a much higher rent than the old one. Where would the money raised by the government from land rent go? Why to 'Concorde' and to ripping out the centres of fine old cities to build motorways through them and to paying the salaries of more and yet more 'officers' - *taxeaters* as Cobbett so well named them. In any case, a tenant never farms so well as an owner-occupier. You can tell tenanted farms as you drive about the countryside - they are the ones with no fruit trees near the house (why should a tenant plant for the future?) and a general look of comfortless desolation about the homestead. They show a lack of love - why should a man love a home that is not his? 'Give a man an acre of desert and he will turn it into a garden,' wrote Arthur Young, the great agricultural writer of the early nineteenth century. 'Make a man tenant of an acre of garden and he will turn it into a desert.'

Nature's conservatives will say: Leave land ownership as it is. Now in the country I know best, England (I leave Wales out of it now - the state of affairs there is quite different) land occupation seems to me to be unfair, untidy, unseemly and grossly inefficient, (inefficient, that is, for making people happy and for the well-being of the land and the creatures on it). Much of the land of England belongs to huge landowners who let it out to tenants and take as big a proportion of the profits in the form of rents as they can without actually making the tenants go bankrupt. The more traditional landlords themselves only care for *pheasants*, for their social standing in their peer group depends entirely on how many of these silly birds they can 'show' at the five or six 'days' they have on their estate every year. In the moorlands, grouse take the place of pheasants, and in the Highlands, deer.

Increasingly, though, since the war, land has passed out of the hands of the traditional game-preserving squires into the hands of big commercial landowners – often corporations. Possibly this trend may continue, hastened occasionally by a prod from a Conservative government (Labour has shown itself to be consistently on the side of the squires – possibly because most successful Labour politicians become squires themselves as soon as they can afford to) in the way of more anti-evasion measures for death duties and the rest of it, and hastened by the tendency of enormously wealthy industrialists to invest their money in 'land' and pretend to be 'farmers', having of course their 'farms' farmed for them by professional agents. At all events, more and more productive land is now owned by huge commercial landowners of one kind or another. Some small family-owned farms still exist, and their production-per-acre is almost invariably above average, although their production-per-man-hour is low and their profits-per-acre are low too. But in a hungry world it is production per acre that counts.

Now it would take a book, and a long book too, to discuss the pros and cons of huge-scale mechanized and chemicalized farming, and I shall discuss farming in another chapter of this book. But I wish to say here that huge-scale farming is the most harmful development that has ever happened to the land of England or any other country.

The best structure for land-ownership in the country, and in any country in the world, is full untrammelled ownership by an owner-occupier who owns sufficient land for his modest needs. Only the owner-occupier is going to lavish that care and love and sweat and tears on his land that will keep it and improve it for future generations. Only he is going to plant trees and hedges, is going to strive to improve the humus-content of his soil – its 'heart' as the old farmers used to call it, is going to be able to farm it effectually when the oil and the artificial fertilizers and the pesticides and herbicides begin to run out. And supposing he *enjoys* it – supposing he *enjoys* working twice the hours in a day that his city counterparts do - and takes a pride in his holding - is that really such a bad thing? The advocates of huge-scale farming seem to feel that there is something morally wrong in the fact that the small husband-man enjoys his work. One of their great catch-phrases (you will read it at least once in every issue of the *Farmers Weekly*) is 'farming is no longer to be considered as a "way of life". It is a business now like any other.'

And in the cities - let us unearth these faceless fellows who 'own' the land on which our cities stand. Let us find out their names, publish their rent-rolls, discover how they came by it all. The student or working man living in a bed-sit in Earl's Court hasn't the the faintest idea who 'owns' the land under the house in which he ekes out his wretched existence. He is not even aware that anybody does. He is not aware that a very large part of the rent he pays every week goes straight to that faceless 'landlord' who is already so monstrously rich that more money can only do him harm.

A true Socialist government, or a Liberal government, would immediately set about expropriating the city landlord, pure and simple. The agrarian policy should be 'land to the cultivator' and the urban policy should be 'land to the occupier'. Rent for land should become a thing of the past, for *no man ever made the land!* I do not say that the student in the bed-sit should not pay rent to the owner of the house for his room. For someone *did* make the room.

How can we free the land again, for the fair use of all mankind? The Danes did it very effectively by the establish-ment of their *Statens Jordlovsudvalg*, or Government Land Law Board, in 1899. This proceeded to buy up and partition large estates into small holdings. A law to stop anyone from owning more than two farms prevents re-grabbing by land-lords. The smallholdings are nominally still in the ownership of the State, but the occupier has complete freedom, and can leave his farm to his heirs or anybody else. Before he sells it in his lifetime, though, he must obtain the permission of the

Statens Jordlovsudvalg. This is to prevent the big land-grabber – the *bullfrog* as Cobbett called him – getting his greedy hands on it again.

The result? In Denmark there are now about 200,000 holdings and very few of these indeed are tenanted. All but a handful of exceptional cases are owner-occupied. Nearly half of them are very small – under 25 acres (10 hectares), just over 80,000 are between 25 and 75 acres (10 to 30 ha.) and about 20,000 are between 75 and 150 acres (30-60 ha.)

And the result of that? Danish farmers can whip English ones in their own market with any product they like to send them. Danish agriculture is perhaps the least subsidised in Northern Europe, their agricultural exports are quite unsubsidised, and yet the poor old British farmer (there are two hundred British farmers with over *6000 acres* each!) just cannot compete with them.

I have travelled extensively in Denmark and I never saw a bad farm. The land is almost monotonously well farmed. If you only have twenty-five acres you have *got to* farm it well! Or you will starve. Every farm I saw grew a large variety of crops (no monoculture), had a variety of stock (therefore the land will continue to grow crops if artificial fertilizer gets too expensive), had a comfortable farmhouse, (and often two because it is the custom for a farmer to retire early into a second house on his land and the hand the farm over to his son). Every farmer I saw was fairly prosperous, worked hard (which is another way of saying that the production-per-man-hour was low) and the production-per-acre was very high. There is a Danish song which says: 'Few have too much and fewer still too little!' I submit that that is what every country on Earth should try to achieve. We should all be able to sing that song.

How can we achieve this state of affairs in the rest of the world?

There is a very simple way in which it could be achieved, and one proposed by Henry George, the American economist we have already mentioned. It is: tax the land. Tax, that is, not the land itself but the landowner. George advocated the *single tax*, one tax and one tax only, a tax on land value. He claimed that this was the one absolutely fair and equitable tax, because any man who owns more than his fair share of the land of his country should pay, and be pleased to pay, the rest of us for the privilege. The landless man now has a legitimate grievance. He can say – and no-one can refute him – 'it is not fair that some people should have more than their fair share of the land and I should have none'. No one can answer that complaint. It is *not* fair – no argument on Earth can make it fair. But if you can say to him 'yes but the people who do own more than their fair share of the land have to pay a tax on it, and you get the benefit of that tax' – then you can answer this complaint. The tax on land value is thus completely fair, and also it is the one tax that could be devised that no-one could possibly evade. For you cannot hide the land! Governments could sack ninety-five percent of their Inland Revenue Departments right away were the single tax system adopted. Existing Valuation Departments would put a value on every piece of land, the tax would be fixed upon each category, and thereafter collection could be an affair of checking off on a map. Just as no man ever made the land so no man could hide it.

Now I would improve on Henry George's Single Tax scheme by making the land value tax a *graduated* land value tax. This would be based on the theoretical principle that a man who owns his fair share of the surface of his country would pay no tax at all and after that the more a man owned the more he would pay *per acre*. Thus a man owning, in England as an example, five acres of average agricultural land might pay nothing, a man owning twenty acres might pay two pounds an acre (£40), a man owning forty acres might pay four pounds an acre (£160), a man owning eighty acres might pay eight pounds an acre (hence £640) a man owning a hundred and sixty acres might pay sixteen pounds an acre (thus £2560), a man owning a thousand acres would pay £100 per acre – thus £100,000.

Thus a good commercial farmer in the world today owning a hundred acres could very easily pay his land value tax and have plenty left over for himself. A man owning two hundred acres would find himself seriously considering selling half of it. If he did not sell half of it he would be driven to farming it very intensively indeed. He would have to, to pay the land value tax. In other words he would have to abandon high-production-per-man-hour and low-production-per-acre farming in favour of very high-production-per-acre farming. He would have to grow a lot more *food* in fact. To put it vulgarly he would have to piss or get off the pot.

And the man owning a thousand acres would find himself dumping nine-tenths of it on the market as though it were a hot potato. He might keep the other hundred acres and become an honest farmer at last.

The results of this tax would be immediate and dramatic:

1. It would drastically reduce the cost of land. This would mean that anyone who wanted land, and had the industry to save quite a small amount of money, could get some.

2. It would at a stroke end the pernicious 'landlord-tenant' system: a system which has never done anything but harm to the countryside and which never had any basis of justice or equality. It has never been based on any principle except force. There is nothing that the landlord can do for the tenant better than the tenant could do for himself if he did not have to pay rent.

3. It would ensure the fullest possible use of land. Everyone owning enough land to make a living out of it would have to farm it very intensively.

4. It would collect enough revenue for the country's real fiscal needs without resorting to other taxes, which are nearly awlays taxes on enterprise and initiative.

5. It would spread the ownership of the country much

more widely throughout the community. This would be fairer, would give happiness to more people, and eventuallly lead to better use of land.

6. If accompanied by reform of the planning laws it would halve the cost of housing.

Man-made improvements to land should not, as far as possible, be taxed at all. Only the land that the improvements are on, or in, should be taxed. If a man builds a house, it is his. No-one has a right to tax it. If a man drains a marsh the improvement that his draining has made to the land should be his. He should be taxed on the value of the land before he drained it. If a man sinks a mine, it is his. We all of us 'own' the minerals that are under the earth, and the miner should pay the community a tax for the privilege of extracting them, but for the mine itself – the plant and tne hole in the ground – he should not be taxed a penny.

The tax on land is the one tax that is perfectly fair. It is wrong to tax a man's income, for by doing so you are taxing his effort. It is wrong to tax a man's goods for again you are taxing effort. But a tax on land is fair because it is a tax on privliege – the privilege of owning more of his share of his country than the rest of us. The tax would ensure that only people who could make the best use of large holdings of land could hold on to them, for only they could pay the tax.

There would no doubt be attempts to get round a graduated land-tax by the greedy – using 'men of straw' to pretend they owned the land in small parcels while all the time it was owned in a block by one wealthy man, but it would be the easiest thing in the world to nullify these efforts. For the land cannot be hidden. Companies and corporations owning land would be treated as what they are – collections of individuals, and the individuals in them would be taxed, personally, on their total land-holding, whether land they held was in their own names or a share of a corporation's holding.

City land is a question I have no competence to discuss, for I am not a city man, and countrymen should no more interfere in city affairs than city people should interfere in rural affairs. But I am sure that the principles of land ownership would prove to be the same, and that city people, once they had accepted the principle of a graduated land tax, would very quickly devise a way in which it could be implemented. If this were done, it would send the cost of city land plummeting, abolish rents, lower the cost of every manufactured article, and allow the profits of enterprise to go where they belong – to the worker and the capitalist.

The only person who would feel aggrieved from all this would be the landlord. But he would not really suffer, in fact he would benefit. For he would be forced to work at an honest trade and no longer live off the backs of other people. He would recover his self-respect. He might still go on being a landowner of course, for like the rest of us he would be able to retain a reasonable share of his former lands tax free, and pay only a small tax on a slightly larger holding. He could well retain enough land to start an honest business on. It is quite wrong to *blame* the big landlord for being a landlord. He is merely playing the game according to the rules. We must change the rules.

The Marxists chose the wrong villain when they depicted the Capitalist as the man with the enormous belly, top-hat and cigar. The Landlord is the man who should have been carrying these appurtenances. The honest capitalist is a useful man. He is simply using the accumulated product of Labour working on Land to get together the capital equipment to ease the work of himself and his employees and/or to increase their effectiveness (for producing goods). When he gets too big he is a menace, but we have already discussed that in this book.

No it is the landlord who should be drawn with the fat belly, cigar and top hat. Henry George put it something like this (his words were not, I hope, immortal, because I hope that in a few generations the very word landlord will have faded from our vocabulary – as the thing itself will have faded from our society):

No Man Ever Made The Land!

Every blow of the miner's pick, every stroke of the husbandman's hoe, every heave of the sailor on a halliard, every passing of the shuttle across the loom – pays its tax to the Landlord ...

I can already hear one great objection swelling up from the urban masses – who spread out into the countryside every fine weekend in their motor cars – to my proposals.

There will be no *wilderness*, they will say. If we do as you want – break up the great estates either by the imposition of a tax or by any means and establish a country of small peasant proprietors – there will be no unfarmed, uncultivated country. The present squires, in their addiction to pheasants, do at least preserve some of the country as wasteland and woodland.

There are two answers to this. One is that the birds, bees and butterflies and other forms of wild life have more *covert* for themselves (this word means their natural environment) in the varied flora and habitat of a peasant-owned countryside than they do in our existing agri-business barley-prairies where they have no covert at all. The modern agri-businessman is busily engaged in rooting out what few hedges or pieces of copse or woodland as are left to make more and more room for his thousand horsepower tractors. How *else* can he farm with virtually no labour?

The other answer is that after the imposition of my tax (or Henry George's tax to give it its true authorship) far more rural land would be dumped on the market than could be immediately absorbed by buyers. After all, not every townsman wants to leave his nice warm flat and go and be a neo-peasant in the countryside. In fact very few of them do. There would be land, it is true, for everybody who really *wanted* land, but if all the big landowners had to dump all but a little of their land on the market at once, there would be far too much for the market to absorb.

This would be taken care of by a government body (or better still local authority bodies) which would be set up to buy, at the going price (which would be minimal of course) all such land

and hold it for two purposes: one as a wilderness area in which all animals including humans would have the right to roam, to camp, and to enjoy themselves with an absolute minimum of silly rules and regulations enforced by self-important officials. The other purpose would be to be held in reserve for people to buy when the market could, in fact, absorb it. As much wilderness could be retained as we required.

And obviously the graduated land value tax (all right – let's invent a set of initials for it if that makes it respectable) – the GLVT – could be brought in gradually, so that the whole process could be a gradual one.

And nor need we shed any tears for the poor landlords thus forced to sell their land for far less than its present market value. After all, they've had plenty of time since 1066 to squeeze the last drop of blood out of both the land their ancestors stole from us – and us.

And what can we – you and me – do to obtain that the land of our countries is divided up more equitably among people? Legitimate political action is at the moment almost totally unavailing. In my own country of England-with-Scotland-Northern-Ireland-and-Wales-attached it is obviously no good trying to lobby the Tory party to bring about land reform, and as we have seen the English Labour Party will never bring in any measures for land reform for the simple reason that every Labour candidates hopes, when he gets elected and starts enjoying the fruits of office (company directorships and all the rest of it) to buy an estate himself and becomes a landowner. Even Nye Bevan, that darling of the Leftists, became a big landowner – in England too, as far away from the valleys as he could get. Every piece of rural legislation brought in by a Labour government has been more reactionary than Tory legislation. It was the Labour government that upped the fine for poaching a pheasant to fifty pounds for the first offence. Well, after all, our Labour cabinet ministers rear pheasant don't they – and shoot them too.

Well, apart from voting, what can we do? Shout our heads

off about it! I would like to see a society set up in every country called 'Who Owns the Land?' A society set up to inquire into the pattern of ownership of the land, how the land first came into private ownership, who owns it now, what rent they get from it, what they spend the money on, and many other things. When these facts have been unearthed I would like them to be made known and shouted from the hill-tops. I would like every landless man in the world made *aware* that he is landless – made aware of the injustice of it – exhorted to stand up for his rights. These are: *either his fair share of the land surface of his country or its equivalent in other benefits.* And I would like it made quite clear to the big landlords – Cobbett's *bullfrogs* – what the rest of us think of their living off the backs of other people.

Meanwhile, just for fun, I would like to see a great gale blow up one day – maybe on 'the People's Holiday' when thousands of poor devils of factory and office workers are snatching the chance to get out into *their* countryside to fill their lungs with fresh air – and I would like to see that gale of wind blow down – yes and smash to matchwood – every 'Tresspassers will be Prosecuted' notice, and 'No Fishing', and 'No Camping', and 'No This' and 'No That' and 'Private the Other-thing' notice in the country.

Every man has the right to the privacy of his own house and a reasonable-sized pleasure garden (shall we call that the fourth of the Rights of Man?) but no person has the right to keep his fellow citizens off vast acres of their own country. I remember when I came home after the war to England. I had just spent six and a half years in the mountains of Ethiopia and the jungles of Burma and other insalubrious places, fighting, as I had been told, for my country. I landed one day on Skipper's Island, in Hamford Water in Essex, which had been one of my favourite playgrounds when a boy. I was immediately ordered off the land by a man who told me it had been bought by a judge. I left him in no doubt what I thought the judge could go and do with himself.

CHAPTER 6

Chisels Men's Hands to Magnify

I met a man on a mountain in County Kerry, in Ireland, digging peat in the sunshine. Peat-digging is a summer job, a job at which a man can work as hard, or as gently, as he likes, stopping from time to time to listen to the larks or the peewits singing, to wipe the sweat from his brow and survey the splendid mountain scenery around him. As he works he is conscious that he is working for himself and his own family. As he heaps the turfs out to dry in the sun he can see in his imagination the fires of winter that cheer the evening, cook the stew, and bake the soda bread.

I stopped to talk to 'your man' and he told me this was the last peat he would ever dig.

'Why?' I asked.

'Me brother is after gettin' a job with the Coal Board in England, and He drives a machine that'll pick up sixty-five ton of coal at a stroke! Now here I'm thinkin' of him and I cannot go on fiddlin' about with a shovel that'll lift at the most a few ounces.'

So he was leaving his family and was off to join his brother in England.

Later, as it happened, I was doing research for a coastal guide book in Northumberland, and I met one of the drivers of Big Geordie, the National Coal Board's great American-built dragline, in the open cast workings at Radar North. The driver told me that his work was boring, unhealthy, monotonous and repetitive. While he was doing it he told me he only thought of one thing: the money he was going to get at the end of the week.

Now your man on the mountain had to work many days to lay in enough peat to warm and cook for his family for the year. Yon Geordie in the Big Hole could, in one swipe, pick up a year's coal for twenty or thirty families. Therefore you may say there can simply be no comparison in the *efficiency* of the two methods of winning coal. (You have broken Seymour's First Law but for the sake of the argument we will let that go).

Well I think these two methods of winning fuel need to be very carefully compared. I don't think the question is anything like as simple as it appears at first sight. Even the plain crude money-economics of it are not anything like as clear-cut as they seem. The mountain-man was operating with a spade which could well have been made by a village blacksmith and it might have taken that blacksmith a couple of hours to forge. The steel it was made of might well have been made by a small team of men working in a small Black Country foundry. The implement was not, in fact, beyond the powers of an Iron Age culture to produce, and similar instruments were indeed made by the peat-digger's Iron Age forbears. Probably the tool had taken half a dozen man-hours of labour to make, a few pounds of iron ore, some charcoal to smelt it with, and a stick.

Big Geordie on the other hand, although it only had one man driving it, was the work of tens of thousands of men, all of them engaged in more or less boring and repetitive jobs, and most of them living unhealthily in big cities so as to be near their work. It would be tedious and quite unnecessary to try to make a list of what all these jobs were, because anyone can imagine such a complexity for himself: the manager, under managers and heads of departments, the typists, the welfare officers, personnel officers, liaison officers and a hundred other kinds of 'officers', the trade union officials – to say nothing of the actual workers. Suffice to remind ourselves that Big Geordie probably contains material from a score of countries: steel from North America where it was made, copper from Africa, tungsten, chrome, half a dozen other metals and alloys, rubber from Malaya, a dozen kinds of synthetics, and that above all it swallows, every day, a colossal amount of oil from Saudi Arabia. And draglines don't last long – not nearly as long as Celtic shovels. Therefore the differential in *efficiency*, measured by the terribly over-simplified yardstick of the businessman – *money* – is not so great as it might at first appear. That man in the driver's seat of Big Geordie has a back-up of many thousands of other people whom we do not see.

Surely we are too intelligent, though, to measure things by that grossly oversimplified method of the businessman – does it make a money profit or not? It would be unfair to point out that in fact the owners of the dragline under discussion make a thumping loss every year (which they do) for this is outside our argument. Many another dragline owner makes a thumping money profit. As for your man on the mountain – we cannot say whether he was making a loss or a profit, for money never entered into his transactions, except when he or his forefathers paid a few pennies for the spade. All we can say about him is that he was working in the sunshine, on a perfectly beautiful mountain side, at a quiet and healthy job, digging peat for his family. If we like to compare the time economics of his brother on Big Geordie and himself – well his brother on the machine was then making something in the region of £40 a week (heavily taxed and mulcted for 'national insurance') and if his family's fuel consumption was like most other peoples he was having to send home £90 a year to buy coal and another £65 to buy electricity for cooking and heating. Thus he was having to work about four weeks in the year to buy fuel for his family. Your man with the spade did not have to work so hard or so long to cut enough peat to supply the fuel needs of *his* family. We will not compare the enjoyableness of the two means of obtaining fuel for the family because – using as we are the economist's or businessman's yardstick – we are not allowed to consider any other factor except money.

If we do, however, go beyond this and consider other factors besides money we find that the mountain man was completely healthy, for his body was doing what our bodies were designed by natural selection to do: working hard in the fresh air and being nourished with good natural food. The dragline brother was almost certainly heading, as is the nature of dragline operators together with lorry drivers and other sedentary big-machine operators, for a gastric ulcer – if, indeed, he didn't have one already. Instead of good, fresh, home-grown food the dragline operator was living on canteen food – chips-with-everything, the everything coming from tins, packets or the deep freeze (*try* a meal in the next works canteen you come to!) Instead of sitting round a glowing peat fire in the evening with his wife and children singing 'The Wearing of the Green', he was boozing away in a foreign pub, among strangers listening to the hideous noise of a juke box; trying to forget his utter deprivation of anything like home or home comfort and get away from the boredom of living in lodgings in a foreign land. Do you suppose the Big Geordie driver, after a few years of this boring and unhealthy existence, would go home taking enough money to live on happily for the rest of his life? He would not. Talk to the next Irish labourer you meet in England and ask him how many of his colleagues do that. I don't know what happens to their money – *they* don't know what happens to their money – but they don't keep much of it.

Still we come back to the question – how *can* a man go on digging peat happily on the mountainside when he knows that there is a machine in the world capable of picking up sixty-five tons of it at a swipe? If the mountain-man had never heard of the dragline he could have gone on digging peat every summer for the rest of his life and burning it happily in his fireplace.

81

But having heard of it, his own activity – which before had seemed useful and honourable to him – now seems despicable.

Is there nothing between the spade and Big Geordie? It is here I think that we ought to consider the philosophy of Dr E. F. Schumacher, one of the few *real* economists of our time. Dr Schumacher was, as it happens, economic adviser for many years to the National Coal Board, which owns Big Geordie, so presumably he knew something about it.

What Dr Schumacher did, whether consciously or not, was to apply the Law of Diminishing Returns using other ends besides money. He fixed the point at which returns of such things as happiness and health began to diminish at a level of complexity above the spade but below the giant dragline. What about a small petrol-driven machine that a man can handle, costing say, £150, that could be owned by a small co-operative of farmers, and that would cut each man's peat requirements in four days instead of four weeks? There are many pros and cons to be thought of here. It is not so pleasant working a petrol-driven machine as it is working a spade. With the former you cannot hear the larks sing, and that is a very important factor, though no businessman would consider it for one split second. Petrol is likely to become more expensive. But even so, it might be a sensible compromise to make. If there were a giant, all-wise computer somewhere that could be programmed with *all* the factors that bear on this problem – factors such as health, happiness, civilization, mental tension or absence of it, emotional stress that comes with working in huge organizations, the desirability of working in the sunshine, of hearing the larks sing, of men being near their own families, of men being their own masters, of men seeing the beginning, middle and end of their labours – then I am quite sure this paragon of a computer would come up with an answer much nearer the Celtic shovel than Big Geordie. Well maybe we already *have* such computers. Maybe they are called human brains – illumined by a quality to which I have given the initials O.M.C.S.: Old Mother Common Sense.

One must have a factory to make petrol-driven peat cutting machines, you may say. Yes, but it needn't be an *enormous* factory. I have already mentioned the factory at Marstal, in Denmark, where a few score of workers produce what is incomparably the best small marine diesel engine in the world. That's what I call Intermediate Technology of the highest order. I would never work in the factory that built Big Geordie for five minutes, but even I wouldn't mind working in the factory at Marstal, for perhaps six hours a day (that is enough for any man to work indoors), among friends and neighbours, and then off and till a big garden, or a small field, or go out in a fishing boat and catch cod for my family and the market. That would be a good life. My all-wise computer would like that.

There are factories in Northern India where they produce single cylinder hot-bulb semi-diesel engines on a village scale. These engines are heavy, slow-revving, not very powerful, hard to start unless you know how, very economical on fuel and they virtually never wear out. They are used for turning the small corn-grinding mills that you get in most big villages of Northern India (where people eat wheat, not rice), for turning sugar-mills (although most are still turned by oxen), for pumping water for irrigation and for other purposes. But milling is their most frequent use. Now this I think is about the optimum level of sophistication for milling machinery for Northern India. You can of course grind wheat in a quern (two stones). This I think is too low on the scale of sophistication. You could send for the very latest thing in vast break-down mills from Europe or America. This is too high on the scale, and yet that is probably what the orthodox economist or 'adviser' would advise. That is what, in fact, the 'blind workings of the market' will one day bring about. It is more 'economical' they will tell you, to make machinery in a huge factory in Pittsburgh or Coventry and ship it to India, than to build a simple engine in a village factory. Economy of scale, specialization, build-up of 'know-how' – all the rest of it you know. The Indian villagers will thus have time to grow more wheat than they can eat, will export some of it and so get foreign exchange to pay for the mill.

But what if the economists start feeding other factors besides *money* into their computers? Will they get a different result? This book is not about aid for developing countries, and I do not want to go into the benefits of labour-intensive but low-capitalized work for developing countries. Dr Schumacher has, in his books, dealt brilliantly with this. I merely want to subject the question to a *real* cost-benefit analysis, with the benefit part of it taking in everything that affects human beings – and that is not only money. Money is important, it is useful, it is one of the noblest inventions of Man, but it is not everything. I believe that if we do this analysis we shall come up with an answer somewhere between the women grinding wheat with a quern and the huge mill in Delhi or Karachi. It may well be the little village factory working away producing hot-bulb semi-diesel engines. On the other hand it might be a windmill, perhaps one of some new design. It needs a lot of thought, and the application of O.M.C.S.

If the blind workings of the market are allowed full sway, no doubt the little factory will go bankrupt and the villager millers will turn to Pittsburg engines. Then they themselves will go to the wall and all milling will be done in big city mills. The strictly logical outcome would be for us to end up by our having only one enormous mill to mill all the corn in the world.

Well I submit that we humans must interfere with the 'blind workings of the market'. We are not blind! Why should we allow ourselves to be pushed around by any 'blind work-ings'?

The energy now being devoted to research into stupid and damaging things like super-sonic aircraft and flying to the Moon should be devoted to research into Intermediate Technology. Why can't I get a cheap, efficient (for reaping corn), quiet, reaper-and-binder to cut and tie up my wheat? Research into reapers-and-binders stopped when the combine harvester was invented. I don't *want* a combine harvester – it costs about six thousand pounds. If I cut my wheat with one I should have to invest in expensive grain drying and storing equipment too. I don't want to cut my wheat with a scythe either. I haven't got time and my wife and children haven't got time to come along behind me and tie the sheaves up anyway. The old-fashioned reaper-and-binder is heavy, cumbersome, fragile, hard to maintain and killing for a pair of heavy horses to pull. Furthermore you can't buy them any more. Given modern technology it would be possible to design a machine of perhaps half the weight, half the draught that would do the job better. What about having a horse-drawn machine with a fractional horse-power motor on it to drive the cutter bar and binding machinery. A horse is very efficient for pulling things if the things have no driving wheels. Such a machine would be very light for even one horse to pull and would burn an almost negligible amount of fuel oil. It could also be made in a small village factory, as many of the old reapers and binders were. We could make the world's oil reserves last many centuries by the use of such technology. But the 'blind workings of the market' won't take *that* into account. The 'blind workings' will use up our oil, in a few decades.

The title of this chapter comes from a line in a poem by George Bottomley called *To Iron Founders and Others*. The poet imagines men searching about among the rubble of great iron and steel works, after these have collapsed into ruin, for the metal to make 'chisels men's hands to magnify'. I think that line sums up very well what we should require of our tools, machines and implements. That they should magnify the power of our hands. When machines make use of men we have a state of affairs favourable to machines but devastating to men. We men should remain the masters. We should use our naked hands where possible – but when *we* decide to we should fashion ourselves tools and simple machines to magnify the power of our hands just enough (and no more) to gain for ourselves the good and seemly life, with a minimum of setting up of huge, boring, and life-denying organizations. We should never let the end out of sight when considering the means.

What are the ends of industry? Why to provide that everybody willing to work has good food, shelter, clothing, the possibility of travel if he really wants it, and the simple tools of culture: books, musical instruments, paint and canvas, a few simple things like that. These ends are quite simple to achieve – they require only the simplest of means. They don't need Pittsburg, or Big Geordie, or Concorde, or fools flying to the moon.

By allowing big business to have its way we have lost sight of the ends because of the awful complexity and all-pervasiveness of the means. We are like a man who wants to plant a hundredweight of potatoes in his garden. He goes to his neighbour to borrow a wheelbarrow to carry the potatoes in. The wheelbarrow has a puncture, so he has to go to another neighbour to borrow a pump and a puncture repair outfit. He spends the rest of the day doing this and mending the puncture and the next day finds it is pouring with rain. He had better have humped the sack on his back and carried it down the garden path in the first place.

There seems something in our human nature that makes us too much the perfectionist. We start off with very few and simple ends: good food, shelter, clothing, travel and culture. We develop more and more complicated means to achieve those ends and before we know where we are complexity has taken over. Ordinary honest bread is too coarse for our oh-so-delicate palates and the same principle applies to all our other foodstuffs. We have to have everything refined and whitened until it isn't really food at all. A simple house with four walls and a roof is no longer adequate for us – we need some complicated 'machine for living' with every imaginable gadget to 'save labour' (but these gadgets in fact all make more labour than they save – for hubby has got to work in that horrible office or factory to *pay for them*). When we travel, we are not content to get our bodies from A to B but must have every imaginable and non-imaginable refinement to cushion us from the effects of having our bodies flung about in space faster than the speed of sound. A simple and beautiful life in this so beautiful world ends up a complicated and unending hassle, in which our planet is ravaged and Mother Nature insulted and shamed. She may not put up with it for much longer, either.

Let us by all means have tools, machines, implements for different purposes, but let us subject each machine to a sharp and searching scrutiny to decide just where – on the scale of complication and sophistication – diminishing returns set in with regard to such factors as fun, contentment, health, mental health, as well as money.

Of course if economists – just orthodox money-economists – really did their work they might come up with results very different from the ones they do produce. For example, supposing each industry in a huge city was debited, really made to pay, for the cost of the increase in physical and mental illness caused by big cities and big industry. Would those industries still 'pay so well', would they still seem so 'efficient'? Or if they were landed with the increased cost of crime prevention that big-city life makes necessary? Or garbage disposal? Or traffic congestion? And all the rest?

I know it is not a simple exercise to decide just where returns of such things as health, happiness, beauty, safety, lack of harm to other species, fun, spiritual well-being begin to diminish on any scale of size and complexity. To find out the best implement on a scale running all the way from a spade to Big Geordie is not a simple calculation bearing all those factors in mind. It is easy enough for the money-economist or the businessman. After all, they have only to consider one factor – money. They don't even have to consider that very far – no further than the direct effect it has on their own enterprise or business. If we have to consider scores of other factors, desirable and undesirable, we cannot leave the sum to anything so crude as a computer, even the biggest in the world.

Nothing less than the human brain will do, and the best kind of human brain at that – one that can make its owner laugh, or weep, or be angry, or shout for joy. The most elaborate computer that will ever be constructed on this or any other planet will only be able to tell its owners what they want to be told.

My brain, miserable specimen of its kind though it may be, tells me that diminishing returns of all good things set in well short of the Big Geordies of this world. It also tells me that once the Big Geordies have been built they take on a life and appetite of their own. Right, we have this enormous capacity for gouging out fuel. We must use it! And so we must increase our demand for fuel! We must build up a huge advertising industry – to force down peoples' throats the things that fuel can make! We must go far beyond the satisfaction of the simple needs that all men have for we can only use up all that coal, oil and atomic energy that our huge and elaborate machines can produce for us by travelling ever further, faster and more frequently, and finding ever more elaborate ways of enjoying 'culture' (it ceases to be real culture when it becomes too elaborate). Our shelter must become ever more elaborate – so hot in winter that it nearly suffocates us – so full of gadgets that running a home is like driving a space machine – so full of 'comfort' that we become like grubs in a cocoon and lose the use of our backbones. True we can't *eat* more than our bellies will hold, but by God we can waste a lot, and we can ensure that what we do eat is processed and packed and advertised and carted enormous distances and distributed in a way which makes the most demand on Big Geordie and his pals.

Why go to the pub next door when we can 'jump in the car' and travel to a pub twenty miles away? True it's no better when we get there than the one next door, but what's the fun of just walking to the pub? We've got that fast car – we can afford the petrol. After all oil just bubbles out of the ground, doesn't it? The government has built that smooth straight road, knocking down I don't know how many people's houses to do so. So off we go.

The truth is that Big Geordie and his pals are no longer our servants now. They are our masters. They call the tune and we dance to it. They are not chisels men's hands to magnify. We are the chisels.

CHAPTER 7

Nanny Knows Best

I am not an Israelite, but I find the ten laws that the Jews claim were given to Moses on Mount Sinai quite adequate and all that there ought to be in the matter of laws. The terrible proliferation of laws, rules and regulations over the last century is a direct result of having countries that are far too big to manage themselves in a reasonable manner, and also of the power-seekers' firm belief that they know best.

I have just had my application form to register for Value Added Tax, a new imposition that has been put on the people of the British Isles, who now slavishly follow the other members of the 'Common Market' in all bad things. I have yet to meet one person who approves of this new tax, or in fact who does not think it pernicious and damaging in the extreme. If the country voted on it I would be very surprised if ten percent of the votes were in favour of the tax. Increasing as it does the cost of *everything*, it is the most inflationary measure ever introduced. Its introduction led immediately (as any fool could have seen it would) to a leaping of prices for every commodity and a mad, though justifiable, scramble on the part of all trade unions for more pay for their members.

The purpose of the tax is to allow the government of the day to interfere with every little detail of our lives. If the government thinks that ham is better for us than bacon – then it can whop another ten percent on bacon or take ten percent off ham. (Don't worry – it would do the former not the latter). At present the government is playing it rather carefully. They are still afraid there might be a tiny spark of spirit left in the country. When that spark has finally been stamped out they will begin to manipulate.

Of course the government must do *something* to raise the money to finance their exorbitant projects. Alisdair Fairley, in an article in *The Listener*, stated that in 1973 a man with a family earning £2,328 a year paid annually:

£98 on war or preparation for war
£82 on retirement pensions
£65 on schools
£55 on hospitals
£33 on roads
£20 on Northern Ireland
£20 on supplementary benefits
£20 on capital spending by local authorities and new towns
£20 on general practitioners
£20 on local authority health and social services, sickness benefits, etc.
£15 on police
£15 on universities
£15 on grants for depressed areas
£15 on housing subsidies
£10 on family allowances
£10 on refinancing export credit
£10 on non-military foreign aid
£10 on subsidies to farmers
£10 on tax collecting.

The same man today may earn twice as much but the

proportion of his income he spends on each of the above remains fairly constant.

Fairley points out that in that year this typical British taxpayer paid £2.73 on Concorde and a munificent £1.49 on the Arts. Well the Arts have never done me any harm if they have never done me any good, but Concorde for years now has been sending its shock waves which frighten my lambing ewes, cause my cows to abort and bring the plaster down inside my porch. Being part of the Celtic Fringe I may be safely ignored by anyone conducting an objectional experiment – after all we Fringers don't have many votes.

If anybody came up to you in the pub and said: 'Look old boy – we're having a little whip-round, don't you know. Your share of it will be two pounds seventy-three new pence this year but next year it will be more of course. It's for a fine cause though. It's to build a flying machine to take very wealthy businessmen from London to New York in two hours less time than they can be got there now. *You'll* never be able to afford to ride in it yourself of course and every time it flies over your head it will make a shattering noise. It uses a vast quantity of fuel and it pollutes the atmosphere. What would you say to him? What would your reply be? Would your hand shoot into your pocket to haul out two pounds seventy three new pence?

Well nobody asks you for this money – Nanny just takes it from you. Because Nanny, of course, knows best.

I think the whole list that I have reproduced above should be subjected to very close analysis – not by politicians, who have a tremendous interest in preserving the status quo, but by the rest of people who have to pay the taxes.

I make about £2,328 a year when I'm very lucky. Do I really want to spend £98 of it on keeping a standing army in Germany? I do not. I don't want to spend twopence on keeping a standing army in Germany. I cannot conceive that that army is doing anyone in the world the slightest good at all by standing in Germany. £98 is an awful lot of money for me to have to shell out on something that can be of no possible benefit to me or to anybody else. Of course if you asked Nanny what the army is standing there for she would answer: 'To stop the Russians.' To stop the Russians from doing *what?* That piddling standing army wouldn't stop the Russians from doing anything.

£82 on retirement pensions? Well if my working life is forty-five years I shall have paid, at that rate, £3740 on retirement pensions, plus compound interest on the sums paid. This latter will have brought it up to an enormous sum – enough to pay a score of peoples' retirement pensions. Of course I realize that a great deal of this colossal sum goes to paying the salaries of the army of 'officers' administering it all, and paying for *their* retirement pensions. I don't want to pay any retirement pension tax and I don't want any retirement pension. If any man exercises ordinary thrift during his working life (and if he is not debarred from access to land by an unfair land-owning system) he will stash away ample wealth to retire on. If he doesn't – then to Hell with him – why should I subsidise his stupidity?

I would like to see the £65 for schools being used to break up the huge corner-boy factories that are currently turning out the next generation of delinquents, and to replace them with village schools where the children would at least be happy.

What of the £55 spent on hospitals, £20 on general practitioners and £20 on local authority health services? Well, if people lived simpler, more frugal and harder-working lives, working manually that is, you could cut that lot by three quarters. All disease is caused by expecting our bodies to operate in conditions for which they were not designed by natural selection. We were designed to operate in fresh air, in heat and in cold, to use our muscles hard, to sweat a lot, and to eat a varied and natural diet. Keep a man indoors all day, sitting down, feed him on emasculated over-refined food like wrapped sliced pap and white sugar, fill him with anxieties about his 'job' and his 'career', make him breathe petrol fumes every time he goes outside – and of course he gets ill. And then

I, who never get ill, have to spend £95 a year on hospitals and medical services. If hospitals and doctors and chemists were fee-charging I would, in my life so far, have spent just about this sum on myself and my large family.

£33 on roads. Fairley points out that this is ten times what is spent on subsidising public transport. Now if say half of this £33 was spent for a few years on arranging ways of shuffling goods and people around other than on the roads, or better still not shuffling them around at all, we wouldn't need to build any more roads and could thereafter incur a modest annual expenditure (raised and spent locally I would hope) to look after the vast network of roads we have already got.

It would be tedious to go through the whole list here. But I think every citizen should go through the list for himself and think very hard about it indeed. It is far too serious a matter to be left to politicians. After all, they are not affected by it, except in so far as they have the fun of squandering the money. For they are the only people who can give themselves a rise in salary whenever they feel like it. And, as we have seen in the last few years, they have no qualms about doing just that.

Of course the whole monstrous system grows with what it feeds on. Value Added Tax raised £3454 million in 1975/1976 and raises more with every succeeding year. For remember, the £453 that the average tax payer has to pay, as shown in the list above, is only income tax. God knows how much he pays in increased prices because of VAT. What's more, the vaster the sums raised by taxation the more ways Nanny has to find of spending it all. The vaster will be the motorways blasted through our green and pleasant land, the more ruthlessly the centres of our ancient and beautiful cities will be ripped to pieces to make room for 'urban freeways' and endless office blocks, the larger the useless army that will be 'standing' in Germany – and the larger still will be that other 'army' of desk-bound civil servants that will not be standing but *sitting* all over our country, battening off the labour of the rest of us. Why, the VAT head office, in Southend-on-Sea, had 7,700 people working in it the first year and I have just heard that it has been decided to increase the Southend contingent by another three thousand. And that of course is not counting the scattered army of other VAT 'officers' in every city and small town in the country. A new *shadow* army that does not occur in any published figures is also growing rapidly. This new profession is of men who have learnt to wangle your VAT returns for you. We all have to use them now. They, too, have to be fed, clothed, housed, given the means to travel and allowed the equipment of culture.

Have we got to have this sort of thing if we live in a large modern state? If so, then it is not worth living in a large modern state. Let us for God's sake keep things small, straightforward, simple and easy. We have got to have taxation? Well let us have far less of it, and what we do have, let it be locally raised and spent by local governments, on which we can keep a close and pretty baleful eye.

We, the ordinary people have to pay it all, we have to try and understand the officialese and gobbledegook to fill in the endless, mindless forms in a style which can be processed by a mindless machine. One begins, uneasily, to form an impression of what our *real* masters will soon be like. So what can we do about it? How can we break away from Nanny?

I was staggered at the supineness of the British people when VAT was thrust upon them. They all knew it was iniquitous. They grumbled and moaned. Even farmers, whose product is VAT-free, hated and hate it – because they have to claim back the money that is first mulcted from them, which means an awful load of extra work and book-keeping for absolutely no good result. Yet they joined in and paid up! King Charles the First had his head cut off for imposing a tax far less onerous and iniquitous than this one. I would not advocate so extreme a measure for the instigators of VAT (although no doubt the *pheelosopher* sitting in a musty office who dreamed it all up could very advantageously have his head divorced from his body) but it would have been the easiest thing in the world –

would be the easiest thing now – for the British people to bring VAT down flat on its face.

We are told by the aggrieved VAT 'officers' that 850,000 out of a total 4,250,000 forms incorrectly completed in the first year caused great chaos at the VAT offices and nearly brought the whole dreary thing to a halt. What if next year a million forms are incorrectly filled in? What then? It is no longer possible to affect our rulers by democratic processes. The countries we live in are far too huge – Nanny is far too powerful. It is time we began to consider other measures. There are plenty of them.

What about a new religion that makes it a sin to fill up a form? Being made to fill up a form is an insult to our human dignity. The adherents of this religion would say to Nanny: 'I will write you a letter and tell you anything what I consider it legitimate for you to want to know. I will talk to you on the telephone. I will talk to you face to face. *But I will not fill up a form!* I will go to prison rather than fill up a form. There is no information that I can give you in a form that I cannot give you equally well in a letter. I am not a computer. I am not an automaton. I will express myself in my own words – in my own way – or not at all.' What would happen to VAT then, and all the other dreary nonsense that Nanny thrusts upon us?

I remember the Agricultural Training Board Levy. This was foisted on farmers a few years ago by Nanny, in one of her busy-body moods. We were all to pay a levy on the acreage we held, to benefit some mythical 'training scheme' which nobody but Nanny wanted. Nanny wanted it to increase her family – with training 'officers', administrative 'offiers' and all the rest of them. She wanted a huge building put up guess where? – in London, to house them all. Well a small percentage of the farmers of Britain slavishly paid the levy. The greater majority flatly refused. One or two farmers were made examples of, taken to court and fined. Their fines were paid for them by the rest of us and we would have subscribed enough money to pay a thousand fines. The 'training levy' was quietly dropped. Officialdom had seen the red light.

When I came to this farm a scheme was mooted to make us all register our private water supplies. My water comes from a spring on the mountain on the farm above me; where it comes from and where it goes to concerns two people in the whole world: George Hughes who farms the farm above, and me. When I received the form about it, with its mention of dire penalties for those who delayed filling it in, I dropped it in the fire. There were further warnings of dreadful consequences – even the Farmers' Union press uttered them – but in the event over ninety percent of Welsh farmers and over fifty percent of English farmers destroyed their forms. Again, Nanny saw the red light and the matter was quietly dropped. One more little panjandrum had failed to set up an empire.

I have a dear old friend who lives in Suffolk and used to earn his living hauling barges about on the mud, laying moorings, tarring barge's bottoms, breaking them up for scrap, converting them into house boats – things like that. As he got older he used to lie on his sofa for an hour or two in the afternoon, after the pub had closed. I never saw him in my life without a pair of long thigh boots on and a blue jersey, and I like to picture him wearing these garments when the following event occured.

He was lying on his sofa when his wife woke him up and said: 'There's a gentleman at the door. Wants to see you.'

He got up, staggered to the door, opened it, and said: 'What'ye want?'

'I'm – er – I'm from the Inland Revenue,' the man said.

'Don' belong to it!' snapped my friend, and he slammed the door in the man's face.

There should be far more slamming of doors. *A supine people is a forcing ground for tyrants!*

But politicians want *power*. That is why they are politicians. Why they chose their profession. They think they know best. They are convinced the rest of us are incompetent to make decisions for ourselves – they want to make our decisions for us. We are not fit to be entrusted with the wealth that we create: We might spend it on the wrong things. So the politicians try to take as much of it as they can away from us. To spend on our behalf, of course. Government is all a matter of Nanny Knows Best. But demonstrably Nanny does *not* know best, for each new Government introduces policies quite opposed to these of its prececessor.

One of the most blatant cases of interference with our lives is the case of the planning laws. These interfere directly and indirectly with the lives of every one of us, whether we know it or not. The rent you have to pay for your bed-sitter or the price you have to pay for your expensive 'property' are both far higher than they need be because of the planning laws. Further, the price of everything you buy is indirectly raised by the effect on factory and shop sites of our planning laws. The scarcity value of land with planning permission is felt all down the line. If we are all thus taxed, and taxed again, by the planning laws, who then reaps the benefit? Why the land owners of course. The owners of the land which has suddenly been increased in value often by as much as a hundredfold, because of the squiggle of the pen of some 'planning officer'. He is the original Lord Luck. One squiggle of his pen and this man is made monstrously rich, that man ruined. Government is supposed to disapprove of gambling – yet what is this but the wildest, maddest, most monstrous gamble that has ever been invented? A small farmer in my parish was suddenly made immensely rich a couple of years ago by a stroke of Lord Luck's pen, which decreed that he had planning permission to build forty horrible little holiday chalets on his land. Land, for which he had paid twenty pounds an acre suddenly became worth twenty thousand! The farmer next door, equally worthy, whose farm was equally apt to be covered with horrible little chalets, got nothing and still has to go on slogging away milking cows twice a day, three hundred and sixty five days a year and three hundred and sixty six on leap years. The British pride themselves on being relatively incorruptible, but what incorruptibility can stand up to pressure like these? Is it any wonder that a Lord Luck here and there lands himself in goal from time to time? Of course they are only the ones who get found out.

'But if you do away with the planning laws the whole country will immediately become covered with little brick boxes!' I hear the familiar cry. Well it wouldn't. Would more houses be needed then than are needed now? If there is a need then the sooner we allow people to build houses the better, for people *must have houses.* If every family though is already housed and the country isn't in fact 'covered with little brick boxes' then it wouldn't be so covered without the planning laws, for everybody would have a house. Either we need more houses or we don't. If we do then we must have them – planning laws or no. If we don't then the planning laws are redundant. The planning laws can't in the end stop people building houses, for people must have houses. Sometimes they do prevent people building a rash of houses all over good productive farm land. But they also make the people building the houses pay enormous prices for the land they build them on, which money goes straight into the pocket of some land owner who, you can probably bet your life, already has more money than is good for him. The planning laws are a method of taxing the poor to help the rich. True some governments are trying to get in on the act too nowadays and grab some of this artificially-created value, but the result is the same for the poor devil who needs a house.

Before this century there weren't any planning laws. Any man of taste will know that the cities, towns, villages, and country houses put up before the Industrial Revolution were infinitely more comely and beautiful than the ones that are being put up now.

The Town and Country Planning Laws came in in England to stop the terrible rash of jerrybuilding – the awful mock-Tudor pseudo-timber-framing that was spreading like a blight over the land in the Home Counties. This rash was the result of the motor car. It was the result, too, of English country people having been forced off the land that was their birthright to swell the already swollen cities. Cities were made intolerable by weight of numbers so that subsequently their inhabitants wished to flee to the open air again. With their native good taste lost to them, cut off from all their traditions, is there any wonder that these swarming thousands built houses of such abysmal ugliness?

The planning laws did not cure this evil (which still goes on) but they did rather ineffectually treat the symptoms. They were - and are - effective enough to make a lot of big-city people think that they are worthwhile.

But consider the evil that they do! The dreadful, irreparable harm caused to the countryside by forcing all the brighter and younger people to leave it, because they cannot get houses, or establish a means of livelihood. Why these laws, in the end, speed up and exacerbate the evil they were meant to remedy! They force even *more* people from the country into the cities, squeezing city-dwellers haphazardly back into the countryside.

In twelve years of living where I do, in the countryside, I have not seen one existing house sold to a young couple wishing to set up home in it, nor have I seen one case of a young couple being granted planning permission to build a new house in the countryside. Every house that is sold is bought by a wealthy city gent who wants it for a holiday home, or else to retire to. This complaint has been made over and over again, in every corner of our countryside, nobody challenges the truth of it, and yet no-one anywhere raises a finger to remedy the situation! The remedy is at hand. Either force Nanny to abolish the planning laws - or else make it impossible for her to enforce them. Have a law, or a tax if you like, to discourage people owning two houses. There would be sense in that.

I have seen case after case of young people, talented some of them, many of them dying just to stay at home where we need them to bring new life to a dying and ageing countryside, being forced to pack up and leave and go to Cardiff, London or

Birmingham. I am watching this country where I live being stripped of its young inhabitants just as ruthlessly as the Highlands were stripped by the Clearances. My own children will have to go – why should they stay in a countryside rapidly being turned into an unpeopled desert? 'But they can get planning permission to build in the village envelope' says the official voice. Oh? And pay two thousand pounds for a few square yards of rubble to build on? And then be forced, by nonsensical and footling 'building standards' to put up a house far beyond their means? They haven't *got* thirteen or fourteen thousands pound to build a house with. A young married couple who have not yet had a baby can live very happily in something altogether simpler. I would sell a plot of land to any young couple I liked for a nominal few pounds – give it to them if I liked them enough and they could build a simple, comfortable dwelling with their own hands for a fraction of the cost. I've lived happily in all sorts of dwellings, all over the world – including tents, caravans and shacks and it has done me no harm at all. When baby came along they could built a bit on to their home. In five years time they would have made enough money to build a more substantial house. But oh no. Officialdom doesn't like it. So what does a young couple do? Why they go to London and live in a completely insanitary bed-sit in Camden Town, (they are allowed to do this of course "Nanny doesn't seem to mind) until the family breaks up under the intolerable strain and we have a 'Cathy Come Home' situation.

As I write this a young friend of mine who in desperation built himself a house on his own land at Crymych, because he could find no other way to house his family, is having to stand by and watch it bulldozed – and he himself will have to pay for the bulldozing. He will be ruined of course. He will have to slink off and vanish into poverty and anonymity in the city. Never mind – Nanny provides excellent arrangements for taking children into 'Care'.

All healthy industrial development in the countryside is

killed before it is born. A man near here tried to get planning permission to convert the cowshed of the farmhouse that he had bought (the house was divorced of its land, which had been added to another farm) into a small workshop. He wanted to make very specialized surgical instruments, at which he is a world expert. He would not have altered the outward appearance in any way (what if had?) and he would have given employment to a dozen of the young men and girls who hang about the street corners round here. But oh no – there was to be no 'Industrial Development in an Area Scheduled for Agricultural Use'. There is an official catch-phrase or slogan of gobbledegook to cover every human situation. So this small Industry, just the sort of development we need, was destroyed. Yet a huge American oil company was recently allowed to put up an enormous oil refinery bang in our national park. That was all right, somehow. An official of CoSIRA, the ridiculously named successor to the Old Rural Industries Bureau, allegedly set up to foster industry in the country, told me that his work was constantly being thwarted, because every time he approved a scheme to start a rural industry and was willing to give a grant to help it, planning permission for the workshop was refused. The First of the Rights of Man should be: the right to his fair share of the land of his country or its equivalent in other benefits. The Second: the right to build a house on his own land. The Third: the right to work in his own home and on his own land.

You cannot make people good, or give them good taste, by passing laws. Interference in our private affairs never has the result that it is intended to have. The cunning and venal find ways to get round the laws, and to cash in on them, while the rest of us have to pay for it.

We should mistrust all government, all the time. The less of it the better. Until we have administrative units of a sufficiently human size for us to be able to exercise proper control over the servants we pay to run them, then we must reserve for ourselves the right of non-co-operation. The present vast bureaucratic moloch can only exist because of our co-operation. Withdraw this and it will crash to the ground. We don't need to resort to violence. We don't even need to break the law. Passive non-co-operation with officialdom would be quite enough

It would be nice if there could be a democratic solution. Voting Peoples' Party in England, Plaid Cymru in Wales, Scottish Nationalist Party in Scotland, the Cornish Nationalist Party in Cornwall, might one day help. But we must make it quite clear, even to these people, to whom we think 'power' should belong. Not to our servants anyway. But the very word 'power' has a sinister ring. It would be nice to see power, and the lust for it, become a thing of the past.

Every member of every government in the world should be made to read a copy of Orwell's *Animal Farm* at least once a week, and there should be a huge notice up in every council chamber and government office saying: *Don't be pigs.*

CHAPTER 8

Agriculture:
the Basis of Our Existence

Ever since the Neolithic Revolution, farming has been incomparably the most important of the activities of Man (except, of course, procreation). It is quite separate and distinct from what we nowadays call Industry. I remember the Scotsman who taught me the bogus science of Economics at Wye College saying: 'It is wrong to talk of "Industry and Agriculture". We should talk of "Agriculture and other Industries".' Well I think we should not. We should not bracket agriculture with industry at all. Agriculture is something quite separate and distinct and far above every other creative activity of man. To call a farmer just another industrialist is nonsense; a farmer is the most important man on Earth.

I am not talking, be it noted, of the agri-businessman. He is an industrialist. His role is purely extractive. He is simply extracting the fertility of the land that has had the misfortune to fall into his hands, and converting fertility which has been mined from the Earth or extracted from the air by the use of power, itself removed from the Earth, into inferior food, so that he may make a profit. The differences between the farmer and the agri-businessman are sharp and distinct. The farmer, or husbandman, works with nature, not against it, and he obtains from the land the food and other material that he requires without either impoverishing the land or importing large quantities of matter from outside the holding. His aim is to maintain or increase the fertility of his land without importing much from outside.

The agri-businessman, on the other hand, has no regard for the permanent fertility of the land he holds – he merely uses the ground as a base to hold up his plants. These he feeds with imported chemicals, sprays to combat the inevitable disease, and keeps from weed-competition by more imported chemicals, which have been designed to do the crop less harm than the competing weeds. Lest there is some city reader who has never driven out into the country and looked about him, and therefore doubts what I say, here is a description of the 'farming' methods of an agri-businessman on the Essex coast, described in the *Farmer and Stock Breeder*, July, 20th 1974.

> This is what happens. Straw burning starts as soon as there is a safe space behind the combines at harvest. Then a 145 hp County 1454 goes in with a heavy 3-tine Doe-type cultivator to pan-bust down to 14-15 inches. Working at a rate of about 30 acres a day this operation is often right up behind the combines. This is immediately followed by a 100 hp County 1004 pulling two sets of discs in tandem or, if the soil is too hard to disc, a Lantrac chisel cultivator. (*Note the enormous expenditure of power right through the operation. J.S.*) ... The last weeds are killed off in early October with paraquat at the full rate of 1½ pint an acre. ... It would be wrong to think that it's minimal cultivations alone that have solved a sticky farming problem and created a streamlined and profitable enterprise. As stated at the beginning of this article, this has only been achieved by a total commitment to chemicals as well.
>
> The move to a five-year run of winter wheat brought with it all

the expected pest problems, and some more besides. Most noticeable was the build-up of wild oats and blackgrass. These two weeds are now being severely bashed by Dicurane in the autumn and by Suffix in the spring - both sprayed over the entire acreage for two years running. The paraquat used in September must also get rid of some seedlings ... Another problem has been aphids ... this year half the acreage was ground sprayed with formothion.

In their coastal situation, the wheat crops on this farm are also particularly prone to ear diseases such as Septoria. It is thought that these diseases, plus the inevitable mildew have kept average yields to below the two-ton mark. An attempt to reduce the effect of these diseases was made this year with an application of Benlate and Maneb on 400 of the 2,500 acres.

The reporter (John Parry) announces proudly that the entire enterprise - 2,500 acres of some of the best land in Europe - is operated by six men.

Now it would take a book, and a long book, to discuss the pros and cons of large-scale mechanical-chemical farming. I merely have room to say here that it is the most harmful development that has ever happened to the Earth we live on. It is bull-dozer farming, chemical-warfare farming, Belsen-house farming: farming at which the agri-businessman is *at war* with nature, at war with his land, at war with the countryside. All those chemicals listed above (six of them), are toxic and untried by more than a few years of use. Indeed they have only been in existence for a few years. The agri-businessman's whole philosophy is kill, kill, kill. He can suffer nothing, whether animal or vegetable, to survive on his land if it cannot be turned directly into profit for him. His concern is *not production per acre*. Labour is by far the greatest of his costs and his concern is *production per man-hour*. He would far rather produce under two tons of wheat with machinery and chemicals than over it with the help of men. He would rather grow half a ton of wheat per acre and make a money profit than two tons an acre and make less profit, or a loss.

Agri-businessmen are fond of giving figures to show how production per acre of different crops has gone up in the last hundred years. If this has really been done, it has been done only through the acquisition of enormous amounts of chemical fertilizer. The quotation above makes no mention of the huge quantities of 'NPK' dumped on that two thousand five hundred acres every year – nitrogen, phosphate and potash. The nitrogen is won from the air with great expenditure of power, the phosphates and potash mined out of the Earth in other countries and brought in to this one at great expense of foreign exchange.

I know that Essex countryside, and I will bet that in the high farming days of the last century that land produced two tons of wheat per acre. Cultivated by horses, tended by men, nothing was imported for it from outside except, perhaps, occasional lime. There was proper rotation of crops and the feeding of a large number of animals, with the subsequent spreading on the land of their dung. The wheat straw, instead of being burned, was trodden under the feet of the wintered cattle to form dung. A quarter of the acreage every year was given over to nitrogen-fixing clover, and another quarter to growing a *cleaning crop* – a root crop which had to be hoed and which thus controlled, very effectively, the weeds. Of course it was hoed by men.

It has now been convincingly shown that the quality of foods grown using massive applications of soluble nitrates is not so good as that of crops grown on a balanced, organically alive soil. But this apart, can it really be supposed that man can go on, century after century, dosing and swamping the soil with toxic chemicals – which have to increase in virulence as time goes on and the various living things they are intended to destroy develop resistances to them – and not eventually feel the effects? What of the social consequences of such farming, and the effect on the landscape in which we all have to live? The article I quoted shows a photograph of a Landrover standing three miles from the farm buildings, with nothing but a wheat prairie stretching as far as the eye can see. What sort of a country is this? No people, no children playing, no trees, no hedges, no houses: this whole enormous stretch of England does nothing but turn huge quantities of expensive oil and chemical into wheat of questionable quality. It provides a bare living for only six men who do nothing else all their lives but drive tractors over a boring landscape, and it makes one man enormously rich. Is this really a good use of land? Two thousand five hundred acres of land of this quality could support four big villages, fifty prosperous farmers and their families, each of whom would have more land than the average Danish farmer. It could support a large head of stock of every variety and provide a substantial amount of varied food of the highest quality, for export, without requiring the importation of an ounce of pernicious chemical. Further, that land could be a beautiful place, with orchards, garden, spinneys and shelter-belts, and a wide variety of plant and animal life. *And the Lord took man and put him in the Garden of Eden to dress it and keep it.* Not to turn it into a huge wheat prairie, with nowhere for birds or small wild animals to live and the very earthworms destroyed by noxious chemicals.

Chilean nitrate of soda (the accumulated droppings of seabirds in a rainless climate) pushed corn yields up towards the end of the last century, but it also started European agriculture on the slippery slope of dependence on 'bag nitrogen', with consequent neglect of sound husbandry practices. Chilean nitrate is now used up, but nitrogen extracted from the air by electrical power (using ten tons of coal-equivalent to produce a ton of fertilizer containing twenty percent nitrogen) has taken its place. Because initially it was cheap (because power was cheap – didn't it just bubble out of the ground?) It came into greater and greater use. Well the peak seems to have been reached. In England the average yield of corn per acre is now going down. As John Parry noted in his article on the Essex agri-business, yields – on that most magnificent wheat soil – fail to reach two tons an acre. Now

Arthur Young, Cobbet and other agricultural writers of the late eighteenth and early nineteenth centuries were constantly noting yields of two tons of wheat per acre, and that was before there was any 'bag nitrogen' at all. Then, nothing was put on the land except lime and farmyard manure. Nothing was sprayed and disease was unimportant. Spurred on by cheap nitrogen, yields have undoubtedly gone up (*three* tons of wheat is not unknown nowadays) but the peak was reached some years ago and is unlikely to be reached again. The curve of yields of wheat in Northern Europe is now downwards. This is partly because of the depletion of the soil of its humus content, and such of its constitutents as cannot be replaced from 'the bag'. Even more alarming though, are the swiftly growing depradations of a score or more of insects, fungi, bacterial and virus diseases that, in spite of all the armoury of a vast chemical industry, are becoming increasingly harder to combat. At the South Eastern Agricultural College, to which I went forty-five years ago, I learned all there was then to know about diseases of wheat. Now there are so many new ones, then unheard of, that I have given up trying to keep track of them. I grow wheat on my little farm and, provided I start with clean seed, suffer seriously from no disease at all. My contribution to the chemical industry is nil.

Land cannot, in the event, support high arable farming decade after decade on machinery and chemicals alone. Even the *Farmer's Weekly*, the most ardent machine-and-chemical advocate of the lot, has been forced in the last decade to issue warning after warning about the dangers ahead; and so has the usually rigidly conformist government advisory service.

Whereas the old-style English farmer fatted a hundred bullocks on his couple of hundred acre arable farm, feeding them entirely on his own farm-grown produce, and turning all his straw into valuable manure under their feet in the yards in which they were wintered, the modern agri-businessman *burns* his straw. All East Anglians have heard the new-style agri-businessman boast 'I haven't got a four-footed thing on my farm!' You only have to travel around the corn belts after harvest to see thousands upon thousands of acres blackened as though the Huns had ravaged them, all that remains of the thousands of tons of good straw which should have gone back into the land as humus. Why is it burned? Because farming without labour makes it impossible for the farmer to keep bullocks (hence the terrible price of beef); if a person does keep bullocks he has to keep them Belsen-house-style with no litter under them at all. If you try to plough stubble with the straw lying on it your plough and becomes bunged up and you can't do it. Some large scale, self-styled 'organic farmers' are currently trying to develop machines for chopping up straw behind the combines so that it can be ploughed in. But true organic farming cannot be conducted on huge farms. If a man really wants to become an 'organic farmer' he must take a small acreage that he can really manage in an organic way, and farm it with the hands of men, not machines and chemicals. The straw-chopper is simply trying to cure the evils of machinery with more machinery, and this never works. Another reason for straw burning is that it is one method of destroying weed seeds and disease organism that are the result of monculture and bad husbandry.

The trouble is that the large-scale mechanized agri-business-man, because of his scale and high capitalization, has been forced above all to be a specialist. If you have to pay twelve thousand pounds for one combine harvester you can't afford to keep chickens. The one thing you must do above all others is to save labour. The question the agri-businessman is for ever asking himself is: 'How can I dispense with another man?' The result of this has been to divorce the stock from the land. The animals have gone to the Belsen-houses, far away, where they are exploited (I cannot bring myself to say looked after) by another agri-businessman who has no land of his own. The stockless land is farmed without animal manure. What happens, you may ask, to the animal manure which is, after all, still produced in the Belsen-houses? Well it has to be disposed of – very often dumped – at great expense. It is filthy stinking stuff anyway, bad for the land if it is not carefully composted or treated first, for it is just raw shit. In Belsen-houses the animals and birds are kept without straw or other litter. They are kept on wire, slats or bare concrete, hosed down every day; their droppings, which should be a blessing, are a stinking embarrassment.

When the next agri-businessman tells you 'only we scientific agriculturalists can feed the millions in modern populations' *do not believe him.* He and his like will, if not prevented, end up by starving the millions. Their land is running out under them. Their production per acre is on the downward curve. They are bankrupt of ideas of good husbandry.

What if the fuel does run out, or become even more prohibitively expensive then it is at present? The one thing the agribusinessman is prodigal with is *power.* He is hooked on power. He needs two things: fuel to run his machines, and chemicals to kill weeds, destroy pests and diseases, and to fertilize his debilitated soil. These chemicals are made with *power.* Nearly all of them in fact are made from oil, so if oil did become much scarcer than the result would be catastrophic. Imagine what would happen to that farm on the Essex marshes if suddenly oil became too expensive for it to be economical to work all those hundred-horsepower tractors, to make all that hideous list of chemical warfare substances and, above all, to produce the vast amount of fixed nitrogen without which none of that wheat would grow! What would that agri-businessman do? Could he suddenly rustle round and find horses to plough 2500 acres? He would need at least 150 of them, men to work them and farmyard manure to bring back life to land? He would require at least twenty tons an acre of farmyard manure to start off with, so that's fifty thousand tons of the stuff. Where would he suddenly find the men and women to hoe the six hundred or so acres he would certainly have to put to row-crops to keep his land clean without all those chemicals? A good man can hoe an acre a week and the land would have to be hoed twice every summer, so there we get seven thousand two hundred man-days. I don't see how he could get that hoeing, and second-hoeing, done in time with less than two hundred people.

I met a big farmer neighbour of mine at a ploughing match at the time of the last oil crisis. He said to me, as we watched half a dozen big tractors competing: 'What'll happen to all this is the oil runs out?'

'What will you do?' I said.

'Give up ploughing and spray with Paraquat.' Paraquat is a particularly powerful herbicide that kills everything living on the soil and thus makes ploughing weeds in unecessary.

'And what do you think Paraquat is made of?' I asked nastily. 'Fresh air?' He walked away a more thoughtful man, because Paraquat, of course, is made from oil.

And yet it is possible to produce heavy yields of every kind of crop and animal on the land without the use of any fossil fuel outside power imported fertilizers or chemicals at all. This other kind of agriculture is self-perpetuating; it does not exhaust the soil but brings it to a high level of fertility and keeps it there. This kind of agriculture could go on until the end of the Earth and never damage the land. But to farm like this you must be prodigal with labour. You must get men and women back on the land, and animals too. You can do this in two ways: either by retaining large farms and having hired men to work on them, or by having small farms worked by their owners and their families. I submit that the latter is by far the happier arrangement. It is nice to be the owner-occupier of a farm. It is not nice to be a farm labourer. Further, an owner-occupier will work much harder than a hired labourer, because he *enjoys* doing it. I love working on my farm. When I am not writing I love doing it, and no day is ever long enough for me.

Money-economists often say: 'the revolution in agriculture that has brought in mechanization and chemicalization means that each piece of land produces a bigger *net* export of food, for there are fewer people actually working on the land, and therefore fewer mouths to feed on the land itself.' The silly fellows forget that, when you have displaced all those people from the land, and sent them to the towns – *they have still got to eat!* It doesn't matter whether they do their eating on the farm or in a city – they still eat just as much. If you brought them all back to the land, admittedly the net output of food from the land would go down but there would be fewer people in the towns. At least the same amount of food would be produced, and probably much more.

Another argument against re-establishing a peasant agriculture is that peasants are poor, overworked and ignorant. If you go to some peasant countries you will find that indeed they are: but if you go to others (Denmark is a shining example amongst many) you find prosperous, hard-working and well informed peasants. For sheer brute ignorance I'd like to commend to you some of the big-scale agri-businessmen. I know. The most intelligent people I know happen to be neo-peasants.

Another argument against townspeople going back to the country is that 'the countryside would be covered with horrible little brick boxes.' As you travel about England or the United States in your horrible little *tin* box, are you really enchanted by what you see after thirty-five years of machine-and-chemical farming? Does your heart warm to the square mile upon square mile of dreary, treeless, hedgeless, houseless, flowerless barley-prairie that today is East Anglia, the Wiltshire Downs, the grain lands of the Midlands, or Northumbria? You cannot get out of your car in such country – except to sit on the narrow strip of verge or in a 'layby' inhaling the fumes from the tin boxes of other middle class motorists. In such areas there is no longer any common land that you can wander over, no pasture land, no woodland (except little blocks with 'Trespassers will be Prosecuted' notices all over them): nothing but miles of ploughed land in the winter, monotonous green corn in the spring, standing corn which you must certainly keep out of in the summer, and blackened burnt stubble in the autumn. Bird life and animal life are almost entirely absent. Do you really find this so enchanting? Does this remind you of the England of Constable, or Gainsborough, or Chrome, or Cotman?

So what do you do? Why you go to Italy, or Spain, or France for your holidays. And there you find a countryside so beautiful that it takes your breath away. Terraced hillsides growing grape vines, olive groves, small fields of corn surrounded by high poplars, other fields growing a great variety of crops: a stand of tall maize here, a block of dusty-grey globe artichokes there – vegetables and herbs and trees of all sorts carefully husbanded and tended to be of benefit to man or beast. *And the Lord took man and put him in the Garden of Eden to dress it and keep it.*

We don't, when we go to France, linger in the huge corn belt of the North which is farmed, English style, by large-scale agri-businessmen.

What makes the difference? Why people! The beautiful areas of the world are the peasant areas, where human hands, directed by human brains, dress and keep the land lovingly. You can only act lovingly to a piece of land if it is yours, and will be your children's.

We can never achieve this beauty, this rich fecundity and variety of life, both plant and animal, ay and this high production of good food per acre from the unaided land without getting human beings back on to it. I know the agri-businessman sometimes achieves high yields – but any fool can turn expensive oil-based chemicals into inferior food on any land.

The time is ripe for change. Thousands of people who have been through the big-conurbation stage of development – what I call the pimply-adolescent stage – want to come out of it. They want to get back to their birthright – the land. They want to plant orchards and woodlands and plantations, to build good-looking houses, and till fields which ring again with the voices of children and not just the roar of tractor engines. It will take them years to learn how to do it all, and first they must forget their urban belief that country people are 'simple', and country skills easy. The science of good husbandry is a science of enormous complexity. I have tried to learn it and practice it all my life, and I am sixty, and I am a learner.

CHAPTER 9

The Walls of Jericho

If the conventional 'democratic' cure for our ills is impossible because of the vast size of our political units, how else can we affect society and the world around us, and perhaps play our part in stemming the rush of the Gadaren swine over the cliff? Let us consider a few of the other main activities of Mankind, and reflect how we ourselves, by our individual actions, could to some degree influence them. Remember, our political votes may be useless (unless we vote for some devolutionist party).

There are other ways in which we can vote: with our *purses*, by buying one thing and refraining from buying another; with our *feet*, by walking out of the giant, inhuman factory, office, or city; and with our *tongues* and *pens* by speaking and writing out against Gigantism. We can get rid of interfering officialdom by ignoring it, and by using all lawful means to refuse to co-operate with it, by refraining from taking advantage of the 'benefits' it would confer on us, by bartering with each other, by producing as much as we can ourselves and by learning to do without a great deal of the junk that Gigantism tries to stuff down our throats. Do we *really* need a quarter of a 'giant' package of noxious and polluting detergent to wash up with? Try using just very hot water and a long-handled brush. We gave up using detergent years ago here and our plates are perfectly clean. Detergent wasn't invented fifty years ago and people got on perfectly well. We should try to avoid buying anything that puts money in the pocket of a man who has already got too much. Every time we smoke a packet of fags, eat a packetful of breakfast cereal, open a tin or a packet of frozen food, we are doing just that. If a product is lavishly advertistised – boycott it. *You* don't want to have to pay for all that advertising, do you?

Let us consider some of the activities on which our lives on this planet depend:

Trade. Barter is a lovely idea, but it really doesn't work very often. When I want something from you it generally happens that you don't want anything from me and so the barter system breaks down. But consider my 'little Red Book System'. We each buy a small notebook. You write on one page of yours: 'John Seymour owes me' and on the opposite page: 'I owe John Seymour'. I do likewise, but with your name instead of my own, in my book. Then every time you have some good or service from me you credit me in your little red book and I debit you in mine. You initial my entry and I yours, so there can be no argument. At the end of the year, or when we reach the bottom of the page, or when you like, we tot up what you have had from me and what I have had from you, subtract the smaller from the larger figure, and then one of us pays the other the difference – either in money or in some acceptable goods or service.

Advertising. If people have to be persuaded to buy something it means they don't need it in the first place. It is legitimate to advertise for sale a cow, or a house, or to bring to the notice of the public that there is some new product that might be useful to them. The brainless advertising of cigarettes or soap powder is harmful and ridiculous. Advertisers tell their employers that their activity causes people to buy more of things than they otherwise would. Well what good is done by this? Stimulating an artificial demand for things that people can very well do without or causing the public to prefer one product over another not for reasons of intrinsic quality but because the public is gullible, are not helpful activities. How can we by-pass them? By consistently buying the product that is least advertised, or not advertised at all. By remembering that if you buy a heavily advertised product it is *you* and your fellow dupes who pay for all that advertising – nobody else.

Shopping. Here again we can vote very effectively with our purses. Make it clear to the chain stores that deface our towns and cities with their monotonous bad taste that we don't want them. Indicate that we would prefer to pay more for goods if we can have good-looking shops again, with courteous local people in them, and not hideously ugly, standardized chain-store architecture, brainless assistants inside them who haven't the faintest idea of what they are supposed to be trying to sell, and closed-circuit television cameras concealed all over the place in a vain attempt to prevent pilfering. Perhaps without our voting these horrible places will go broke anyway, because every year, it seems, they are losing a larger and larger percentage of their shoddy goods to pilferers. The trouble is, by the time they do go the way of the dinosaurs, the public will have got into the habit of pilfering, and will carry the habit with them when they return to honest local traders.

We are willing to pay for our pleasures. I would willingly pay quite a lot to prevent the pretty little town near where I live being defaced by such supermarket. Then if I have to pay with slightly higher prices for the goods I buy, I should be willing to pay in that form.

It is a useful exercise to go into any big shop and go through all the things that are on the shelves and consider if they we are really necessary, or even desirable. Some products, indeed many of them, are positively harmful. Detergents are a case in point. We all washed up perfectly happily before they were invented, and then our rivers didn't foam and stink and our stomachs were not assailed by the traces of highly poisonous chemical (a product of the petroleum industry of course – so many of the evils that afflct present-day man come from the oil wells) which has not been thoroughly rinsed away. Most tea in cafés and restuarants tastes strongly of detergent, and yet probably they are told to use the stuff 'for hygienic reasons'. We could do with a lot less hygiene and a lot more common sense.

When we are shopping we should never purchase without questioning very hard whether it is really necessary. After all, food, shelter, clothes, resonable travel and the means for culture are all there is. Look at the junk and rubbish that clutter the shelves of most shops! Plastic ash trays that perch on the arms of arm chairs with a complicated method of swallowing up the ashes, china ducks that fly across the walls, all sorts of kitchen gadgets that are supposed to save labour but actually make it, – because the planet has got to be ravaged to get the raw material to make them in the first place.

Our capitalist economy creates endless 'wants'. It forces people all over the world continually to strive to invent new gadgets in order to be able to turn from being labourers to being capitalists themselves. It causes established firms to do research into ever more numerous new substances and devices and to keep bringing out new 'lines'. Most of the 'lines' that were invented in Victorian times, and were considered so essential then, have been abandoned because it was found that they were not essential at all. Most of the 'lines' considered so essential now will be abandoned in due course for the same reason. But this sort of development (with its subsequent advertising campaigns to pressure people into thinking they need the stuff) is forced on us by materialist-capitalism. Industrialists must expand – or go under. The need for more and more goods, in greater and greater variety, must be stimulated at all times, in order to keep industry going, and

119

'give people employment'. But if people were far more self-sufficient, and far less psychologically dependant on material things, they would not need all this 'employment'. The true labour saving device is the device of persuading ourselves that we don't need so many things. Food, shelter, clothing, travel and culture – that is all there is. If an item in a shop does not fit fairly and squarely into one of those five categories then you don't need it.

The shopper is a very powerful person – much more powerful than the voter, who in present day society can achieve nothing. If the shopper says: 'I don't like vast sums of money being spent on huge advertising campaigns' he can stop it. If he says: 'I think it better to use local produce than to bring stuff from far away' he can encourage local production and stop stuff being brought from far away. If he says: 'I don't like things the production of which pollutes the planet' then he can stop pollution of the planet. If he says: 'I prefer hand made things to mass produced because I think hand production makes for a happier world' then he can stop mass production. The hand that carries the shopping basket, more than the one that rocks the cradle, rules the world.

Education. Education has been drawn into the world of competition so that now teachers and parents alike force their children to vie with each other in a rat race which makes Wall Street look like a church fête. If a coal miner were asked to work a twelve hour shift six days a week he would very rightly go on strike. When my children were at school they worked more than a twelve hour shift. They worked overtime every night of their lives when not on holiday – and even their holidays were spoiled for them by 'holiday tasks'. I shouldn't have allowed it? Well how could I stop it? We did not live next door to A.S. Neill's school (I wish we had) and I would not and could not afford to send my children to boarding school. There were not enough like-minded people *then* to form our own school. But teachers pile all this work on children for if they did not get their 'A levels' and their 'O levels', and all the dreary rest of it, the teachers would get the sack. Parents, in forcing their children 'on' as they call it, are not thinking of making better people of them. They are just thinking of getting them a better competitive position in commerce or industry when they grow up.

If people needed less, produced more of what they did need themselves, used more things produced by local industry and less from the vast conurbations or far countries, were more apt themselves to engage in local small-scale crafts or industries – they would not *need* all these ridiculous 'A levels' and 'O levels'. There is a need for scholars, and if one in twenty or so children feels the desire and has the aptitude to become a scholar then for God's sake give him the chance. To force kids who are utterly unsuitable and completely disinterested to learn a lot of academic information is a lot of nonsense.

Education should be the passing on of the accumulated wisdom of mankind to the next generation. Stuffing heads with unrelated information has nothing to do with it. Children should be shown how to get the information they require when they require it. The main part of their education should be aimed at teaching them the difference between good things and shoddy things, good art and bad art, good music and bad, good philosophy and bad. Their taste and their judgement should be developed above everything else. The stuffing of their heads with a lot of unrelated facts can only do them harm and damage their natural intelligence.

Schools should be small, classes should be small, school hours should be few (a child learns most of what he learns out of class), much school instruction should be done out of doors, teachers should be trained to follow the natural trend of the interest of the children. Gandhi developed the best educational system yet with his Basic Education. All subjects in this system are taught through the medium of handicrafts or agriculture, and the teacher, if he is skilled in the method, does not try to give information to the children until they are naturally ready for it and ask for it.

Basic education in India at its best is marvellous. I studied it at its peak at the teacher-training school at Sevagram. At its worst it is awful, for it demands teachers of the highest quality as *people*, and it seldom gets them. And it has to struggle to survive because in India, as in the West, parents want their children to 'better themselves' – that is to be successful in the competitive scramble for highly paid jobs – and therefore they favour the rat-race type of education.

There is one ingredient that all true education must include if it is to be effective at all, that is love. Love between children and teacher is absolutely necessary for education to be effective. How can you have love in a school of over a thousand children, where the children spend most of their day shuffling along endless corridors between one marvellously equipped classroom and another, being 'taught' by a score of different specialists, everyone of whom is in a rat-race himself and is only thinking of advancing his own career?

Nanny nowadays thinks that good education can be ensured by having expensive and elaborate equipment. These, she thinks, can take the place of love. The equipment in some chemistry laboratories now is so elaborate that even the chemistry master doesn't know how to make it work. What is the good of the vast and expensive 'gymnasium' you get in every school? How can climbing up ropes, etc. take the place of hard work out of doors on the family homestead, or climbing trees, or rowing boats, or scrambling up mountains, for building healthy bodies?

The best school I ever saw in my life was a school in India which consisted of four grass walls, a grass roof and an earth floor. The children sat on the latter and were taught with love and imagination by fine teachers. The best people in every generation should be the teachers of the next – but we should *all* be teachers. You don't have to pass exams in a 'teacher training college' or be a member of some trade union to be able to teach other people. One of my daughters came home from school one day and asked me if I knew the date of the accession to the premiership of the Younger Pitt. I took her away from that school, as being no fit place for my child to go if the intention there was to stuff childrens' heads with a lot of irrelevant and useless nonsense. Shortly before that she had come to me and announced that they were teaching her 'soil science'. 'Oh' I said, 'how many soils have they shown you so far?'

'Oh they don't actually *show* us soils – we do it all on the blackboard!'

The remedy, one that we can actually make use of, is to boycott these educational sausage-factories. Refuse to send our children to them. Oh yes, we can do it quite legally. Form our *own* schools – plenty of people have already done so or are doing so. Form our own schools, teach our children ourselves at home, band together to teach each others' children – refuse to throw them into a juvenile rat-race at the age of six or eleven plus! The purpose of education is to show children the difference between good and bad and to equip them to obtain any information that they may require. Examine the taste in music, art, drama, literature, of the next school-leaver you meet and see if you think the first of these aims has been achieved.

Factories should be as small as they can be and still be able to do the work they have to do. As people learn to live happily with less rubbish, most of the factories we have today will become redundant anyway. As the craftsman comes back into fashion, and takes the place of the machine-minder, most of the Dark Satanic Mills (and their contemporary equivalent – the light ferro-concrete Musak-filled mills) will fall into the ground anyway. In any case it will become harder and harder to get people willing to work in them.

Power: We should want, and need, and use, far less of it, and

123

of course most of it should come from renewable sources of energy.

Transport: The same applies to transport. As countries get smaller, and more self-sufficient, the need to move wool from Australia to Bradford, and suit lengths from Leeds to Bombay will diminish. And the need to move furniture from High Wycombe to Pembrokeshire, or plastic bread from Cardiff to Oswestry, or stale buns from the heart of London to the heart of the country, will go. And for the transport that really is needed – coal or food to London for example, or things that different places really *need* to import or export – then we must ensure that as much of it as possible is carried by water or rail. Even the existing seven-foot beam canals of England could carry a significant tonnage if dredged and brought up to date. The rivers, too, could be made use of much more than they are. A huge timber yard in the heart of Bristol was recently forced to close its shipping quays by an ill-advised city council and now every bit of timber bound for the city has to be carried on polluting, dangerous, and congesting lorries from Avonmouth up the Portway. One would suspect either insanity or corruption in this sort of case if one didn't realise that *stupidity* is what is common to Nannies all over the world.

Packaging. Surely one doesn't have to labour this one? When I was a little boy living in an Essex village, women used to come into the village shop with a number of clean calico bags – one labelled flour, one sugar, one beans etc. The shop-keeper used to fill these from tubs or sacks of bulk produce with a scoop that served also as the container of the scales, and what a good idea! Now everything is packed and double-packed and packed again. A pound of sugar is packed in paper or plastic, and the packs are packed again in cartons, and the whole thing adds up to more trees being wasted (not used for a good purpose which is very different) more oil being pumped up to make plastics, and in the end more work for the dustman to do clearing all this horrible junk away. Carrying this madness even further, the sugar itself is nowadays often wrapped in little tiny packets each holding two lumps. Butter in bad restaurants is served up in horrible little greasy pats, generally slightly rancid, each pat wrapped in metallic paper which is itself worth more than the butter. Of course the utterers of all this filth (the 'packaging industry') do not have to pay for clearing the mess away, nor for the congestion on the roads caused by the stuff being carted about, nor are they accountable to posterity for the desolation caused by the clear-felling and failure to replant the thousands of square miles of forest that every year go as a sacrifice to this mindless moloch. The 'packaging industry' mogols say that packaging is a good thing because it makes more fools buy the stuff packaged than would if it were unwrapped. Gillette, apparently, brought up as a defence of its packaging that the sales of male deodorants have been boosted since the chemicals they are made of were sold in aerosols. Well in this supposed to be a good thing? That more males have been persuaded that they stink so much that they feel forced to spend their hard-earned money on some product that makes them still stink but stink differently?

The Packaging Review announces proudly that the price of the materials used by the packaging industry has now topped the thousand million pound mark in Britain. That makes about twenty pounds a head for each of us. Well I don't want to be mulcted twenty pounds a year to create rubbish, thank you. I want to be included out.

What can the individual do to stop this waste? Well vote with his purse. Buy things in bulk wherever possible. Go back, if you can, to the good old method of little calico bags. Refuse to have everything wrapped up by the shop assistants who have been trained to believe that nothing should leave the shop looking like what it is. There are times when it is convenient, or even necessary, to have things wrapped up but these are very few.

Forestry: Contemporary 'eco-freaks' are obsessed with the idea of trying to collect the direct energy of the sun and turn it into heat or power useful to man. Their means generally take the form of devices stuck up on the roof which will warm, or at any rate take the chill off, their bath water. Arrangements have been made in tropical countries whereby a kettle of water can be boiled, or an egg cooked, with parabolic reflectors, and some experimenters in America have built systems into their houses whereby the heat of the sun during the day is collected and stored to be released during the night. Although there has been much written and talked about it nobody has yet succeeded in storing heat from the sun in the summer for release during the winter to any significant effect.

Because of the great expense of all such devices the area of surface that can be exposed to the sun is minute. A few square yards of roof sun-collector for example costs, currently, a couple of hundred pounds. If you could cover an acre with a sun-collector you could collect a significant amount of power but it would cost more than any individual could afford.

Such experiments are worth-while though, for with new techniques the capital cost may be cut significantly; and it is after all very nice to have your bathwater warmed for you by the sun, or at least pre-warmed before it goes into a boiler.

All such efforts are of course negligible as a method for turning the sun into heat or power compared to the forests. To cover a thousand square miles with a man-made sun-collector would cost more than the combined resources of all the men on the earth but there is many a forest of that extent existing which is already a very efficient sun collector. I have perhaps fifteen acres of woodland on my little farm, most of my artificial heating comes from wood, I cut trees for all sorts of purposes, give people permission to come and help themselves, and I clear woodland for grazing land – and yet in the eleven years I have been here the woodland has grown much faster than I have been able to reduce it. I now have a Norwegian heating stove which burns only wood and which burns it so efficiently that a few sticks will heat a good-sized house for a day. If I could also get a cooking stove (as efficient at using wood as an Aga is at using coal) and a water-heating stove, all my heating needs would be provided by a minute part of the annual product of my woods. In fact the trimmings of my hedges around the fields every year would yield more than enough material. Ninety-nine other families, I would hazard a guess, would be able to be supplied with fuel for their total needs of heating and cooking from my little farm.

The sun fell on forests eons ago, and its energy was ultimately turned into coal and oil. We will one day use the coal and oil up. Then the sun will still fall on forests (as it does now) and we will simply have to use our intelligence to ration ourselves as to heat and power use so that this source of power will be self-perpetuating. With the population of the world as large as it is today I have no doubt that the existing forests and woodlands, properly managed and not squandered, could supply us with all the heat and power that we should reasonably demand. Wood can drive motor cars. In South West Africa before the war, when the Great Depression made money a thing of the past and petrol absolutely unthinkable, the farmer I was working for knocked up a 'producer gas plant' out of sheet iron, stuck it on the back of his Model T Ford lorry, and for years drove himself about on gas made from charcoal. The charcoal was made from the ordinary little bush trees of the veld, and in five years of this the bush hardly seemed to recede at all from the cutting. We also drove a pumping engine from the same source.

Of course there are too many people in the world now. Their numbers will have to be reduced. Reduced they will be, either by conscious restraint on our part, or by controls beyond our influence, such as famine or fuel shortage. If the world held a decent sized population, that is a population that was in some sort of fair balance with the numbers of other species, then we could comfortably and without strain provide all our needs of heat and power from trees. We would not, however, be able to indulge in the frantic and insane spoliation of forests that our present economy makes necessary. As one small example: to read the few square inches of news sheet that you actually require makes necessary the buying of forty pages of newsprint all of which is dumped in the dustbin and all of which is made from timber.

Meanwhile the people of the future, the people who are through the pimply-adolescent stage and are coming back to claim their birthright of land, these will all, one hopes, plant up part of their holdings with woodlands and with groves so that they, at least, will no longer be a drain on the world's fossil fuel reserves.

Let us hope the extractive forestry of the lumberjacks will be a thing of the past. The slaughter of a million trees so that the land is left a barren and desolate wilderness of rotting stumps just so that some rich man can increase his fortune is a blasphemy. So is the fact that the trees, that only God can make, can be turned into instantaneous dustbin-fodder. The paper needs of Man should be as all his other needs: moderate. Apart from lavatory paper (in South Africa we used to use mealie-cobs and I prefer bracken fronds anyway) there are books, like this one, which should be made to last as long as possible, reasonable news-coverage (which means the use of about a hundredth part of the quantity of paper that is used now) and a few other moderate uses. And one day we must cure ourselves of the nasty vice of wrapping everything up.

Meanwhile it would be nice if the 'eco-freaks' got to work and designed a series of wood burning stoves to space-heat, cook, and heat water as efficiently as the coal-burning Aga.

Fishing. When I was a boy I used to spend some summer holidays going fishing in a sailing smack (the *Ida*) from West Mersea, in Essex, with an old man named Bill Clark. We fished with sail alone, towing a heavy beam trawl which was very

hard work to haul in, and I used to get blisters on my hands
and thoroughly enjoy myself. Catches were meagre, and old
Mr Clark only just scraped a living. The *Ida* had an engine in
her belly, but her skipper hardly ever started it. I never
remember fishing with it and only remember it being started a
couple of times when the wind fell away just as we were
approaching home, and the tide was done, and we would have
had to anchor and row home in the boat if we could urge the
old smack on no further.

Skipper Clark used to tell me of the marvellous catches that
he had enjoyed as a boy and young man – right up, in fact,
until the engines had come. After this catches had declined,
because the fishermen had got too good for the fish. The
engines had made the smacks more 'efficient', but efficient, for
the wrong end – destroying fishing grounds.

I have heard the same tale repeated right round our coasts.
Before motors there were many more fishermen than there are
now, all making a living, albeit a hard one, and there were
many more fish. The motors came, along with more sophisticated kinds of fishing gear, and fish, as one would have
expected them to, became scarcer and scarcer. As the fish in the
home grounds were virtually wiped out through over-fishing,
fishing craft got larger, and longer ranged, and fared further
afield. I admit that three hundred years ago English sailing
vessels were sailing as far as Iceland and Newfoundland, but
they went there because in those waters they could be sure of
enormous catches of cod, which could be salted and sold to the
Italians or Spanish, or kept alive in well-holds for months on
end until the ship returned to port. But these ships were not
significantly depleting the fishing grounds. They could have
gone on fishing on this scale (with hand-lines and long-lines)
until the seas dried up, without exterminating the fish.

Now, however, giant trawlers – driven by men hooked on
power just as modern agri-businessmen are hooked on power –
scrape and scour the seas, doing endless and wanton damage to
eggs, immature fish and adult fish alike and damaging the

delicate balance of flora and fauna on the sea bottoms that provide the fish with food.

The oceans are vast, and it seems incredible that puny man could destroy the life in them. But aided with the power provided by apparently limitless and amost free oil man is capable of almost any conceivable mischief. Every thinking fisherman knows he is helping to kill the goose that lays the golden eggs. But what can he – as an individual – do about it? Why absolutely nothing at all. He has got to go on fishing – he is a fisherman and this is the only way he has of making a living. If he went back to selective and non-destructing forms of fishing – the baited hook or the drift net for example – he could not compete against the big trawlers and would go bankrupt. Anyway, what would be gained by his lone stand? The rest of the world would still go on in its destructive course.

And what applies to individual fishermen also applies to nations. Britain, I am proud to say, does try to regulate mesh-sizes, and is seriously thinking of banning the new-style beam-trawl fishing which is ravaging the trawling grounds of the English Channel. It is a feeble attempt but at least it is an attempt. The English fishermen stuck to the selective drift-net for herring much longer than other fishermen who went on to the lethal and indiscriminate mid-water trawl. Eventually the latter engine did something that anyone might have thought impossible: exterminated the vast herring shoals of the North Sea. But, in the end, what is the point of one nation imposing controls on its fishermen when other nations are at liberty to continue their evil ways? I admire the Icelanders in their fight to maintain a fifty-mile limit (although I do not admire them in promptly laying down a large fleet of trawlers to take the place of the foreign trawlers they have banned). But it is obvious, that if we are to go on enjoying sea fish (one of the most thoroughly excellent of foods available to man) we must somehow stay our collective hand from ravaging the oceans.

There are only three things that can happen. The first is that we will go on, nation competing against nation and fisherman against fisherman, until the edible fishes of the Earth's oceans have become extinct. The second is that we will somehow collectively exercise restraint. The third that we will run out of power and be unable to continue our depredations.

The freedom of the sea is a cherished principle, and one for which brave men have fought since they first started going afloat. But freedom must go hand in hand with self-restraint. The time has come, I fear, when the maritime nations must divide up the fishing grounds, so that each nation is faced with the alternative of conserving its fish stocks or going without fish. It is quite wrong that Japanese factory ships are even at this moment, in conjunction with large fleets of trawlers, operating in Irish waters, and that Polish ships are raping the grounds, with small-mesh trawls, a few miles from East Anglian coasts, and that English ships are scraping up what is left of the cod off Iceland and off Greenland. With this kind of unrestricted competition we will very rapidly come to the point at which edible fish have disappeared altogether.

There is, though, one thing that any nation with trawling grounds near it could immediately do, and that without asking anybody's leave or begging anybody's pardon. Old car bodies, of which our society produces millions, are a nuisance and an embarrassment and hated by the scrap dealer. We should drop piles or pyramids of old car bodies (minus their engines of course) at selected points around our coast. Large areas could be chosen and studded with these obstructions, and the positions of these areas made known to the world's trawlermen. Then if they wanted to trawl there, good luck to them. If they went to great expense and trouble of removing the obstructions, then one would simply drop another lot down. They would get tired quicker than we would. In this way large areas of sea-bed would become safe for fish to breed in. Old-type fishermen could still shoot long-lines and crab and lobster pots, and lobsters, of course, would breed in great numbers in complete safety and protection in what to them would be ideal homes.

131

If the power runs out soon enough, the fisheries of the world will be saved anyway. If it doesn't then we will simply have to start farming the sea as we farm the land. Or give up eating fish altogether, and Mankind will have another monstrous and appalling sin on his collective conscience.

Mining and Quarrying. I once went down some graphite mines in Ceylon. The miners seemed to me a very happy lot, and when I remarked on this to the manager he said it was because each one of them had a small farm on the surface, on which he grew his requirements for the year, and only worked underground (on contract) for as many hours a day or days a week as it pleased him. If we must delve for minerals under the soil then this seems to me the be the only decent way of doing it. No man should spend more than five hours a day underground anyway, just as no man should spend more than 5/6 hours a day working in a factory, or an office. It is not healthy.

Mine managers and owners would say that this would be an impossible manner of running things. Well I know that it would not be impossible. I worked for a year underground in one of the biggest mines in the world (Nkana-Mindola) and I would undertake *now* to go over and organize that mine, or any other, large or small, so that each mine worker would have a plot of land on the surface on which he could build a hut or a house, to live in it with his wife or family, working underground for five hours every day, and the mine would not go broke but would prosper.

I was delighted when the coal miners of Britain brought Mr Heath's government down by refusing to continue working eight hours a day underground for less wage than the cocktail barman of the House of Commons gets. I would like to see them strike again – and harder, not for more money but for a five hour day and a piece of land each one, of his own, on the surface to grow his own food on if he wanted to. Who knows what might happen in another hundred years? Coal miners, too, are passing through the pimply-adolescent stage of civilization. Some have already passed it.

Country and Town. Yes – never the other way round. The disease that has brought down civilization after civilization is the disease of the city becoming dominant over the country.

When Cobbett saw a canal being dug in the West Country he inveighed against it, in good old Cobbettian manner, because he saw it as just another channel to take the lifeblood out of the country and pour it into the *Wen* as he called London (what would he call it *now?*) for the sustenance of tax-eaters. The process that he saw and decried has gone on ever since with an ever-increasing momentum. The momentum has now become a panic rush. Cobbett was marvellously perceptive to see the evil and danger of this tendency at such an early stage. He was a century ahead of his time. If we could see the London of Cobbett's day we would say: 'what a fine little city! This is just the size for a capital city to be.' But Cobbett, fine old farmer that he was, could see the huge crop of thistles to come in the tiny seeds of his day and he knew that the Wen, like cancer in the human body, would spread and spread and become more and more malignant until it killed itself by killing its host.

Cities are necessary. We cannot have civilization without cities. But cities must be kept under the control of men, and be pleasant places, there to serve the countryside. City people must feel they have strong links with the countryside. They must not only know – but feel that they owe their lives every day that they live to countrymen.

At present the 'developed' Western nations are ruled entirely by, and for, their city people. Countrymen are ignored. After all, how many votes have they got? they are there to provie cheap food, and bed-and-breakfasts for their masters when the latter make their annual trip in search of fresh air – oh and of course 'jolly country characters' to chat to. The remedy is in the countryman's hands. Don't let them *have* the food that we produce for a little while. Let them sweat for it. They can't do without us, but we can do without them! Let them sweat for it. They can buy cheap food from sweated peasants abroad, can they? All right - make friends with those sweated peasants - *they* have got a National Farmers' Union of some sort too!

But there is a development now that Cobbett did not foresee. He saw the lifeblood being sucked by the new Wens out of the country. But he could not foresee the trickle of this same lifeblood that would, in a hundred and fifty years after his time, be flowing in the other direction. It is only a trickle now, but it is increasing. The people who have *been through* the pimply-adolescent stage of civilisation are beginning to come back to claim their birthright. They are an insignificant minority now. Nanny probably feels she can ignore them. They are bashing their heads against two apparently impregnable brick walls - the wall of land-monopoly and the wall of the planning laws.

But the walls of Jericho were brought down by a shout! This trickle will become a flood, and Nanny will get anxious and try to get these troublesome brats back into the nursery. They won't go and one day Nanny may find herself looking for another situation. Her little charges will have outgrown her.

Two things can happen to Man. He will run out of cheap power. Or he won't. Even if he doesn't, most people do not *need* to crowd into vast conurbations to practice their crafts or professions. If there is a good cheap postal service you don't have to live in the jewellery quarter of Birmingham to be a jeweller. You don't have to live at Stoke on Trent to be a potter. If there is cheap road and rail transport you don't have to live in Coventry to run a light engineering factory.

If he does run out of cheap power, then man will have to de-centralize whether he likes it or not. So either way the trickle of settlers seeking their birthright in the country will become a flood. And Nanny won't be able to stop it, whatever she does.

The country of the future will be a small country, closely allied to other small countries. It will have its wild places but its fertile areas will be closely settled by a skilled, industrious and intelligent peasantry, in a new peasantry of educated and literate women and men. These people will husband the countryside for the benefit of plant, beast and man. They will not rape and exploit it. They will practice a thousand arts and professions to enrich their own lives and the lives of their fellows. They will produce their own good food but will also produce a surplus to feed a modest population in the towns and cities.

The latter will exist as market places and meeting places to serve the country. Young country people will wish to spend some years in a city to meet others and receive the intellectual stimulation that can only be found in the ferment of a city, where many people are within easy reach of each other. The cities will be there to enrich intellectually the country. There will be few city people without close ties with the country. Not a city person but will feel that he has a close tie with some farm somewhere, or country village, or rural community. The day of the lost soul in the bed-sit pining his days away in misery and loneliness will be over for ever.

Art may flourish and develop with a city base but it will spread right throughout the country too. Strolling players will come back into their own again as people turn back to live art from the goggle-box and as country audiences get more intelligent and sophisticated. For two centuries now the country has been drained of intelligent and sensitive people. They have been drawn away into those insatiable urban vortices. They will come back. Men will become full men again. The navvy who can't read a book or the book-worm who can't use a spade will be things of the past. The Holy Trinity of Mind Spirit and Body will become whole again.

'E'en so shall man turn back from violent hopes
To Adam's cheer, and toil with spade again ...'

wrote Quiller-Couch about grooves worn in the stone parapet of a bridge by the ropes of toiling bargemen, back in another time.

We have got to give up the hopes of violent men, the hopes of 'conquering' the universe. How can we 'conquer' something that we are a part of, ourselves?

APPENDIX

A Plan for the Redevelopment of
Dartington Hall Farms on Organic Lines

INTRODUCTION

Although John Seymour's report makes complete sense in itself it may be helpful for those unfamiliar with Dartington to know something of the history, aims and activities which have grown out of this experiment in rural regeneration, launched by Leonard and Dorothy Elmhirst over fifty years ago.

As a young man Leonard Elmhirst had studied scientific agriculture at Cornell from where he went to work with Rabindranath Tagore, the Indian poet and philosopher, who was pioneering village development in Bengal. Tagore believed that Western city-dwelling man led a fragmented life, in which work, education, community, and the arts existed in quite separate worlds. In the fast-moving, secular, urban context he had lost any sense of the underlying unity that binds all beings and things. The revitalization of decaying traditional communities, which still retained the vestiges of old values, offered the only opportunity of bringing all these strands together again. It was Leonard Elmhirst's experience while working with Tagore in the early twenties that laid the foundations of the Dartington experiment.

In 1925 he and Dorothy purchased Dartington Hall, a fourteenth century building near Totnes in Devon, in order to launch an ambitious experiment in discovering ways to restore vitality to the decaying countryside. In the following year they summed up their aims as 'no less than rehabilitation in the broadest sense: not only physical reconstruction and the re-development of all the resources of the estate in contemporary terms, but also scope for a full life for everyone connected with the enterprise.' Thus Dartington has initiated a uniquely broad range of activities in many areas – farming, forestry, land use, education and the arts – all of which were set up in the course of an evolving experiment to revive the physical, social and cultural environment of South Devon. John Seymour mentions the Dartington Hall School, the Dartington College of Arts and the Textile Mill, but there is also a Joinery and a Glass works, book and music shops, a garden, extensive forests, an arts centre with concern for the animation of rural life and departments with responsibilities for adult education, welfare and the care and maintenance of buildings.

Farming on the Dartington estate has always figured large and never more so than in the nineteen twenties and thirties when the Dartington farms were leading the way into a new era. Leonard Elmhirst saw that it was necessary to develop and restore the rural economy along progressive, economic, lines. Farming was, therefore, scientifically run, and combined with vigorous research projects. Mechanization, intensive dairy production, soil surveys, field enlargement and artificial insemination were pioneered and one of the first tractors was introduced into Devon. The new farm buildings included such innovations as continuous roofing, concrete flooring, glazed mangers and provision for cooling and bottling machines. Much of this work had far-reaching repercussions outside Devon. A number of books about the Dartington Hall Trust are available for those who would trace the subsequent development of the Dartington farms and other activities in detail.

In recent years the emphasis has been less on research and innovation than on the commercial running of a predominantly dairying unit of 1,200 acres, managed by a Farms Director, employing a regular force of about twenty-two men. The five dairy herds have a total of 420 cows producing half a million gallons of milk a year. Eighty acres of winter wheat are grown for sale and two hundred and fifty acres of barley and stock feeding.

Yet a future in which we may have to farm without the help of cheap oil and artificial fertilizer looms ahead. Trust has been giving thought to this question and one positive result has been the decision to establish a small educational centre to teach the rudiments of partial self-sufficiency. Yet the question remains: where do we at Dartington, and as a nation, go from here? It is a question John Seymour was invited to answer.

THE REPORT

The Organic Philosophy recognizes that Man is a part of Nature and must work with Nature and not against her, or inevitably both Man and Nature will suffer. The concept of 'The Conquest of Nature' is a false concept and the attempt to put it into practice is doomed to fail, for Man, being a part of Nature himself, cannot possibly conquer Her.

In modern agri-business we have seen the most determined attempt (since the decline and fall of the Roman Empire at least) to 'conquer Nature'. The ultimate aim of the agri-businessman is to eliminate every form of life on his holding save only that one which brings him in direct profit. Thus a wheat farmer attempts to eliminate every bird, beast, plant, fungus, bacterium and virus on his land and grow only wheat. He tries to achieve this by machinery and chemicals. Herbicides will destroy all plants except the one grown for profit, insecticides all insects, bacteriocides all bacteria, etc. As nitrogen-fixing and putrefying bacteria are destroyed their places will be taken by nitrates fixed from the air by the use of electrical energy. As problems arise from the use of powerful and destructive chemicals, these problems are solved by the use of yet more chemicals, the chemist, or the plant breeder, always hoping to keep just one step ahead of the disease (which knows how to evolve too!). This process has gone on until on many a wheat farm in the East of England people are spraying seven times, from the first dose of paraquat to destroy all plant life to the final fungicide before the crop is harvested. As all animals have been elminated, the place of animal manure is taken by huge (and progressively huger) applications of artificials. As all straw is burnt, or removed and not put back, the soil becomes progressively more bereft of humus, but this is not considered to matter because the agri-businessman knows he can always call on the artificial fertilizer manufacturer and he is quite prepared, ultimately, to reduce farming to hydroponics: the soil to be merely a sterile inert substance for holding plants upright while all their food requirements are fed to them in artificial form.

It is the belief of the exponent of the Organic Philosophy that this method of agriculture cannot be sustained, and will inevitably lead to failure and sterility, and the kind of man-made desert that has already been created too often on this Earth.

The method of farming at Dartington is also monoculture but it is monocultural cow farming. It is nothing like so pernicious as the monocultural corn farming we have already described, because here there is a beneficial interaction between plants and animals such as Nature obviously intended (in other words plants and animals evolved together and adapted themselves to interact). The land, which grows the herbage to feed the cows, has the benefit of the dung of the cows, albeit in the less than excellent form of raw slurry. Slurry is nothing like such a valuable addition to the soil as the same quantity of dung would be were it composted with straw into farmyard manure. Also a strict monoculture is not practised with the herbage, for a mixture of grass and herbage is grown, although it is true that in all such leys as are grown for conservation, grass only is grown, because the high applications of nitrates used would suppress any clovers or other *leguminoszae* anyway. Nevertheless, with the system of ley farming practised, with occasional barley crops, and the slurry from the cows, it can be expected that the land will stay in fairly good heart and that land thus farmed will not be turned into a desert. With only one species of animals grazed, and that in such numbers, there are bound to be health problems, but these can be minimized by careful stockmanship (which is very evident), veterinary skills, and rotational grazing.

The objections to the present method of farming at Dartington, from the Organic point of view, are as follows:

Although this is not the Inorganic Philosophy taken to its furthest conclusion nevertheless it is a part of it. It is the divorce of animals from the land in the corn growing areas that has led to dependence there on chemicals, toxic and otherwise, and other violence against Nature. Divorce the animals from the land as has been done (and the Dartington method of farming makes inevitable) and you have the burning of straw in the arable areas on the one hand, and the building up of noxious slurry, and the problems of its disposal, on the other in the pastoral areas. You have an increasing dependance also on high inputs: inputs of chemicals in the arable areas and inputs of imported protein in the pastoral ones, and it must not be forgotten that *all* such inputs either come from abroad or are produced, and transported, with a prodigious use of power, now ultimately derived from either the oil wells or natural gas.

In the era to the end of which we have nearly come, energy has been very nearly free. During this era an economist (who was not also an Organic thinker) would have said that the methods now practiced by the agri-businessman both in the arable and pastoral areas of England were correct. As very cheap energy sources dry up, the economist's assessment will be different. But of course orthodox economists have ever been several decades out of date! They are, like soldiers, always fighting the last war. No doubt there are still some oil and natural gas reserves to be discovered. It may be that governments will have the sense to put a stop to the prodigal and ever-increasing use of power. But the oil companies themselves state that the probable oil reserves of the world are limited, and while it may be a century before there is no oil, there are already signs that there is not so much oil as there was before. There is plenty of coal, *but* somebody has got to go down there and get it; coal will never be the almost free source of energy that oil has been. Atomic power has problems (witness the recent announcements about the Fast Breeder Reactor by the American President). But whether it works or not will never be the source of *cheap* power that oil was. Man will always be able to tap energy sources until the sun goes out but never one as easy as a liquid that bubbles out of the ground whenever a hole is drilled in the right place

The drift toward inorganic agriculture has been the result of a certain ratio between the cost of power and the cost of human labour. Cheap power and dear labour equals inorganic agriculture. Dear power and cheap labour equals organic agricultural methods. The magnificent flowering of organic farming at the end of the eighteenth and the beginning of the nineteenth centuries, the era of High Farming led by men like Coke of Norfolk and 'Turnip' Townshend, when yields of two tons of wheat to the acre were achieved on land which never saw an ounce of artificial fertilizer or a poison spray, was built on cheap labour and not-too-plentiful energy.

The Founders of Dartington, back in the 1920s and 30s, were appalled at the poverty of the agricultural labourer, a necessary concomitant of cheap labour in those days. They determined to end this by reducing the work force on the land dramatically, by the use of what were known as 'modern methods' – cutting out diversity, amalgamation, and the other methods the results of which we see now. The workers displaced from the land were to be provided with jobs by other enterprises which were set up and they had the great vision to try to set up enterprises that made use of the raw materials provided by the land of the estate. It is unfortunate that in the course of time this object got forgotten, and the reason why, I believe, was because of a fundamental misconception of what it was all about. Dartington let itself be pushed about by apparently irresistible outside forces and it followed too slavishly the advice of 'economists' and other theorists who drew their ideas from the nineteenth century. In any case in the nineteen-twenties there really weren't so many other ideas about.

So Dartington, motivated by pure altruism, and acting on the advice of what seemed to be the best thinkers of the time, led the country into the Age of Agri-business.

But we should now consider not the day-to-day policies of the Founders (Leonard and Dorothy Elmhirst), but rather *their ultimate aims.* What were these? As I see it, to bring life, prosperity, and culture back to the English countryside. What can we do best now to further these aims?

If we are to consider this problem in the light of the Organic Philosophy we should first consider just what this philosophy is.

The chief conclusions of it, as I see them at least (we haven't had our Mao Tse Tung yet so nothing has been laid down!) are these:

1. Man is a part of Nature, therefore must work in co-operation with Nature and not against her. As a corollary Man must not try to think of himself as being part from Nature.

2. Nature is diverse. Therefore Man must encourage diversity.

3. All life forms have been evolved by natural selection to flourish under certain conditions. In nurturing them for his own (and their) benefit Man should try to provide conditions for them not too unlike the conditions for which they were evolved. It is often said that we are interfering with Nature by the very act of farming. Is, then, a cow interfering with Nature by the act of eating grass? Or an ant by carrying an aphid up a rose bush so that the ant can 'milk' it as ants do? No, the cow and the ant, being parts of Nature themselves, are not interfering with Nature, they are simply playing their part in it. It is only when we arrogantly assume that somehow we are *apart* from Nature that we outrage her and will inevitably, in the ripeness of time, damage Nature and oursleves. If there is going to be outright war between denatured Man and Nature, I know which side I will put my money on! There is a warlike element in Man's nature, but if he yields to the ever-present temptation to make war on his environment he stands a very good chance of coming off second best!

4. We must obey the Law of Return. We must put back the same amount of low-entropy material into the soil as we take out. (In this context we must remember that everything that has once lived can live again. There is nothing that has lived that, if put in a compost heap, under the feet of bullocks, or dug into the soil, will not provide true fertility to make more life).

5. We must feed the soil and not the plant. There is not space here to go into the complex chemico-physical reasons why this is so (there is a vast amount of literature now on the subject). For the non-scientific it may be helpful to point out that if we spare the soil the trouble of converting what we feed it into plant food, the soil will give up this job and become, in fact incapable of doing it.

In the light of the above principles let us consider what is wrong with the present Dartington farming system, and by extension what is wrong, if anything is, with the rest of the place. How are the laws described above being transgressed?

1. Although the Farms are not as guilty in this respect as many others they are still not really working in cooperation with Nature.

2. The lack of diversity on the Farms does not need labouring.

3. The forms of life on the Farms are *not* being tended in conditions approaching those for which they were evolved.

As a simple, and typical, example of this latter statement let us consider the story of the pig.

A pig is an animal evolved by natural selection to live on the ground, to suffer extremes of heat and cold, to search for its food with its nose and to root in the ground. As it does the latter it eats a good deal of earth. The sow is furnished with an elaborate chain of instincts which come into play when she is farrowing. Days before the event she starts searching for a place to build a nest, she carries straw about in her mouth from one place to another, finally she makes an elaborate nest and has her litter. She then suckles her piglets – and defends them if necessary with great ferocity – until they naturally wean themselves at the age of about ten weeks.

Now inorganically-minded farmers started by taking the sow off the earth, keeping her on concrete, and giving her straw to lie on. It made their work easier. Her chain of instinct was upset by this confinement and she became clumsy and often lay on her pigs. The inorganic answer – to remove the straw and fit a farrowing rail. She became even more deprived and disturbed, her chain of instinct was even more upset, and she began to eat the piglets. Inorganic answer – put her in a farrowing crate where she could not turn round and could only with difficulty just stand up in one position and lay down. Then lure the piglets away from their mother with an infra red light. Apart from the manifest cruelty of this (but Agribusiness has never allowed itself to be deflected by considerations of humanity) it was found that the little semi-orphans became horribly subject to pulmonary complaints (anaemia had been cured by routine injections of iron). Inorganic answer – inject them with this and that, lace their food with antibiotics and heavy metals, keep them at a constant temperature and finally – the crowning obscenity perhaps of twentieth century 'agriculture', the practicing of embryotomy: cutting the living piglets out of the womb of their dead mother in asceptic conditions so as to establish what is known, in the jargon, as a 'minimal disease herd'. And where can we go from there?

It may be of interest here to relate one man's experience of pig keeping in what we can justifiably call Organic conditions.

In 1956 I started keeping pigs and I have been keeping them, with a few breaks, for twenty-one years. I never had less than four sows and generally had six – the latter being the number that will pay the wages of a boar. The pigs were (and are) kept out of doors, but with small moveable, very draughty, huts to sleep and farrow in, and they have always been circulated around the land behind an electric fence. This year we had our first major disaster – one sow died in farrowing and one slipped her piglets. Apart from this our sows have given us an average of twelve piglets a litter, twice a year, and reared an average of twelve, with monotonous regularity. The piglets, at least half of which of course have been born in the winter, have never been medicated in any way, have run out of doors (sometimes with hardly any shelter at all) in all weathers and they and their mothers have had the roughest of food. When we lived in

Suffolk, for eight years, Harvey of Tannington had a regular arrangement with us that he took all our weaners at a pound a head over the market price because he said not one of them ever suffered from virus pneumonia or any other disease. When the terrible outbreak of gastro-enteritis that wiped out most of the weaners in Suffolk occurred, our sixty weaners of the time caught it and the vet said we could expect to lose half if not all of them. We did not lose *one*.

I have gone into the story of the pig at some length because it is such a simple illustration of the way Inorganic thinking works. A problem is cured by an Inorganic solution. This leads to another problem. Cured by another Inorganic solution. And so on and so on. In the end outraged Nature rebels. And what of the conscience of Man? Have we turned barbarians? We made a great pious fuss about Belsen and Buchenwald. Were we qualified to?

4. The Law of Return. In a limited way the Farms obey this law, in a larger way they do not. The farms export low-entropy material in the form of milk and they import low-entropy material in the form of imported protein for the cows and manufactured nitrates to put on the land. They do, however, return the dung of the cows to the land in the form of slurry (there is just nothing else they can do with it!). Composted with straw this dung would make a vast amount of the most magnificent material for feeding the *land* (not the crop) known to Man – but the straw is all being burnt in far-away Norfolk and other places. (Coke of Norfolk claimed that a full bullock yard meant a full stackyard and everybody in those days seemed to think he knew what he was talking about).

5. We must feed the soil and not the plant. The slurry does this to some extent: the inorganic fertilizer not at all. The soil becomes lazy and entirely dependant on inorganic fertilizers as a cripple on his crutches.

The nitrogen-fixing bacteria are absent. The vast complexity of micro-organism that should be present in the soil die for lack of employment. They are not wanted.

I know you can grow *very heavy crops* on such soil with massive applications of chemical fertilizers, but that is not the point. What is the point of turning five calories of energy in the form of fixed nitrogen into one calory of energy in the form of human food – if energy is expensive?

Effect on the countryside of the Inorganic Philosophy

1. The countryside has been substantially depopulated of real country people. The truly indigenous culture has been practically destroyed. Everyone knows this and nobody would deny it.

2. The aesthetic value of the countryside has been seriously impaired. Aesthetic judgements are unquantifiable (most Organic values are) but nevertheless exist.

3. The contribution that the Land should be making to the vital health of the people who live on it is not there. A great quantity of Friesian milk is being produced, taken off to be dumped in with a lot of other Friesian milk (which no doubt contains quite a quantity of both penicillin and mastitis pus – we who have helped milk in big herds know all about this!), pasteurised so as to give it a long 'shelf life', and carted hundreds of miles to who knows where to go down the gullets of who knows whom. And meanwhile where do the people of the Dartington Estate get their food? They buy food (at enormous prices) which was produced who knows where by who knows whom. *The fresh, varied, organically-produced, unadulterated food that they should be getting from the land around them is conspicuously not there.*

4. The vital link that there should be between country people and the country has been completely severed. *There is a Berlin Wall through Dartington. On the one side of it are the Farms, with a small and dwindling number of farm workers on them, on the other side are the rest of the people who live and work on the Trusts estate, in the School, College, and the rest of it.* And the latter never look over the fence! Why should they? First of all what they would see if they did is pretty boring. Secondly they

wouldn't be welcome. A 'Farm Trail', carefully sign-posted and hardly used, is surely one of the countryside's biggest non-events.

5. *The Farms,* even if the milk subsidy was raised, and even if more mechanization, chemicalization, making of more men redundant, etc, is done, *can never be the best possible investment for money in purely financial terms.*

And what if the Farms, run on the present philosophy, were to become highly profitable in monetary terms? Would they be achieving the Founders' intentions? I submit they would not. True, the money they earned could be used for *buying culture* from metropolitan sources. But more money could be raised for this purpose were the farms sold and the money invested in high-yielding industrial shares.

What are the reasons for the failure of the Farms to bring about the results desired by the Founders? The major reason is that the Inorganic Approach (which was at its most rampant in the years between the wars when the Trust was founded) has been followed throughout.

The Inorganic Approach says: 'Big is beautiful'. It worships 'economy of scale'.

The Organic Approach says: 'Small is beautiful'. It is willing to sacrifice economy of scale to a more human scale of things.

Inorganic says: 'Centralize'.

Organic says: 'Decentralize'.

Inorganic says: 'Departmentalize'.

Organic says: 'Treat the whole of Nature and Man and his works as a whole.' Break down barriers between disciplines and sciences. All knowledge is one. There is no intrinsic difference between chemistry and physics, astronomy and geology. *The destructive fallacies of fragmented thinking have been brought about by dividing knowledge artificially into think-tight compartments.* The chemist can only get a chemical answer to any problem, and that probably won't be the right one because *he cannot see the problem in its wholeness.* The same applies to a farm manager, a textile manager, an educationalist, a doctor, a dentist. Everyone, in fact, on Dartington Estates or in the Universe.

You cannot, for example, consider Dartington Hall School in isolation from the land which surrounds it without impoverishing both.

Inorganic says: 'Start from the top and work downwards.'

Organic says: 'Start with the Soil.' The Dartington String Quartet is a product of the Soil just as a bunch of potatoes is, but unfortunately it has forgotten it. And it *should* be far more the product of *Dartington* soil.

The Organic Solution

As an exercise let us imagine what the Estate would be like in *twenty years time* if the right things are done now. Let us consider this in the light of the Organic Principles which we have invented.

Firstly the Farms will be worked in accordance with Nature and not in defiance of her. This means that no *violent* solutions will be imposed on Nature, but the powerful forces of Nature herself will be harnessed to achieve the benign aims of Man the Husbandman (not the malign aims of Man the Exploiter). As an example of this thinking be it noted that Sam Mayall, who grows more and better wheat and gets a better price for it than any other farmer in Shropshire, boasts that he can always show you an example of every kind of wheat pest and disease on his land every summer. You name it – he has it! But he has never, in the thirty years he has been practising strictly Organic agriculture (that is – no artificial fertilizers and no sprays) had his yield seriously affected by any of it.

Secondly, *diversity*. In our Utopian farms of twenty years hence the Farms are growing every kind of crop that can be grown in this climate and on this soil with any hope of success whatever, and there will be every kind of domestic animal. This sort of diversity is essential for Organic agriculture, for every species of plant takes different things out of the soil and puts something back and the same applies to animals.

Further there are areas set aside for wild life.

The third principle is that animals and plants should be kept in conditions approximating those for which they were evolved by natural selection. This aim is easy to achieve under the very rich and varied rotation made possible by the great variety of crops, by the moderate size of flocks and herds made possible by diversity, by the fact that animals are kept out of doors as much as possible (you *cannot* keep a herd of a hundred dairy cows out of doors in the winter!), animals are not 'steamed up' to make them produce unnaturally large yields, animals and plants have been bred for overall health and hardiness first and for yield after. The day of the cow wagged by her udder will be over! As for the methods of the Belsen House and the sweat shop: these will be adjured against for ever.

Fourthly the Law of Return will be obeyed implicitly. *To this end no food will be sold off the Estate until all the needs of all the people living on the Estate have been met in full.* It is so ludicrous that farm produce from Dartington Farms is being sold to wholesalers and marketing boards and that the people of Dartington are having to buy the same products back from retailers that it just does not bear thinking about!

And, most important, all sewage is being returned to the land. This will not be as difficult as might have been thought, nor will it be half as smelly and insanitary as the present system, for the sewage will go straight into methane digesters, together with at least some of the dung of farm animals, the methane extracted to supply some of the Estate's power needs, and the resulting perfectly safe sludge pumped out onto straw beds to activate the breaking down of the straw into farmyard manure or compost. (No fixed nitrogen is lost with anaerobic fermentation of the methane digester: in fact some nitrate that would ordinarily be lost back to the air is fixed into more permanent form. So the sewage after yielding up its methane is more valuable as a fertilizer than it was before). All crop residues

151

will be composted before they are returned to the soil (mostly by being put through the guts of an animal).

Fifthly – that we must feed the soil and not the plant. This is implicit in the type of husbandry that Dartington will be practising. No fertilizers will be bought in at all, and a soil made alive and healthy by years of good husbandry, will be capable of sustaining itself and the crops and animals that are part of it just as Sam Mayall's (and my) soils do today.

In this Organic Utopia the Berlin Wall between the Farms and the rest of the Estate will simply have crumbled away. 'Vertical Intergration' (to borrow a piece of jargon from the gobbledegook merchants) will be practiced with all products all the way. There will be such diversity on the farms, and such close connections between land and people, that this is inevitable. People working in the textile mills will be intimately concerned with the flax growing in the fields and the wool growing on the sheep. Why should they not take time off from their looms to pull the one and shear the other? Workers in the *new* cider press will make sure that this time the *right* kind of apple trees are planted to produce the kind of cider the Devon people want. Children in the school, (forgetting their parents' grisly pre-occupation with the 'kiddies' rat-race) will be fascinated by the great diversity of what is going on around them and no force will be enough to keep them glued to their dreary text books when there is so much that is of interest to occupy them. Instead of their schooling being an interruption in their education it will actually be a part of it! The children will know where their grub comes from and help to produce it. The members of the Dartington String Quartet will become aware of what they are made of, as they take time off to help with the corn harvest or stagger out of the pick-your-own strawberry field. They will not play any the worse for this realization – they may even play better.

It will be realized that this is a low-input agriculture. Therefore, even if little profit is made no great losses can be made either. The workers, who will probably mostly be working in some *cooperative or partnership system*, will derive most of *their* inputs from the Estate (all food and housing for example, and probably much clothing) and will either take this as part of their wages or else spend their money-wages on it, which will thus come straight back to the Estate. The Farms may not be making large book profits – but they will be helping all the other enterprises on the Estate make large book profits. It will be a high-quality agriculture, producing only the very best of every product there is (the insistence of the Founders on the very best of everything is evident from the history) and taking that product to its highest stage of manufacture. And such produce as is not consumed on the Estate will be sold right up-market. It will be labour intensity agriculture and will therefore satisfy the Founder's aim of curing unemployment. As the nitrogen-fixing bacteria of the soil find they are wanted again so will the school-leavers of Totnes and places even further afield.

Decisions in a system of such variety could not all be imposed from above. Highly centralized agriculture in big units is inevitably highly simplified agriculture: hence monoculture. Anything more diverse would be impossible to manage efficiently from one office. The kind of diversity we have at Dartington in twenty years time will require decentralization of power and much initiative coming from the fields or the workshop floor. The Trustees will not say to the manager of the Textile Factory – 'we want you to use wool and flax from our farm.' It is more likely that a shepherd on the farm will say to a weaver in the factory – 'why the hell don't you weave the wool that my sheep produce instead of getting wool from the other side of the country?' The effect on morale of this kind of initiative, this kind of integration, and this kind of diversity will be immense. Gone will be the Great Yawn that so many 'shop floor' workers suffer from in our age from the time they get to the factory in the morning to the time they leave it at night.

As for aesthetics, in twenty years the landscape will have

been transformed. The diversity of crops will give a quilt-like diversity to the arable land. There will be orchards (even *though* this land may not be quite as good for growing fruit as the parts of Kent), more woodland, a delightful diversity of farm animals instead of just two huge masses of black-and-white cows, there will be horses - perhaps even working horses - and most of the animals will be out of doors on one sort or another of free range.

But above all there will be people. It will be a peopled landscape, and the people will be intimately concerned with the land: not just city people out for a 'country walk' or one lonely man in the cab or a huge tractor with ear-pads over his ears to stop him from going deaf.

THE IMMEDIATE PLAN

To come back to reality, what are the first things to be done?

Firstly, anything that does not *pay* is no good at all. Each enterprise may lose money the first year, break even the second, but if it doesn't turn in a profit to the Trust the third year there is something wrong with it. But small splinter enterprises such as we are about to consider cannot be run successfully directly by the Trust, any more than the late-lamented market garden could be, *or the Dart Valley Railway could be run successfully by British Rail. Each enterprise should be the concern of the people running it to the extent that if it goes broke they go broke, and if it flourishes exceedingly they flourish too.* I am not competent to say how this could be but perhaps a partnership between a group and the Trust might work,* or a small cooperative renting from but bound to the Trust by agreements as to the disposal of produce to a greater or lesser degree. (To allow an enterprise complete freedom of marketing would be wrong, because the centrifugal forces would be too

*Crank's Health Food Restaurant, situated in the Cider Press Centre at Dartington, pays an annual rent to the Trust.

great – you would get enterprises selling all their produce to the outside world and be right back where you started from).

Secondly the Organic approach is a slow approach. Start as many enterprises at once as you can but *start them small* and let them grow organically. An acorn is quite big enough to plant if you want an oak tree.

Thirdly use Job Creation labour. This does *not*, as some people have feared, cut across the tender feelings of trade unionists, for the workers get the rate for the job and redundant trade unionists have as much chance of being employed by it as anybody else. We have a marvellous opportunity here to build the future with *free labour*. For God's sake lets seize it! If I can do it here at Fachongle Isaf I am quite sure Dartington can do it too, even though on a much larger scale, but for just the same sort of purposes.

The First Enterprise

Firstly plan to open a food shop (all classes of food) at Shinner's Bridge and another perhaps in Totnes, or possibly somewhere in Torbay. This or these shop/shops will be unashamedly up-market, trading on the current popular prejudice in favour of 'whole food' or 'organically-produced food'. There is not the slightest sign that this prejudice is decreasing – in fact there is every sign that it is increasing. The success of the Whole Food Shop in Baker Street is one of the success stories of late years. And what about Cranks itself? As produce becomes available twist Cranks' arm to get them to use it in their restaurants.

Market Garden. Get some experienced and keen people to start one or more market gardens *now*. Plan to provide every kind of vegetable and fruit that can possibly be grown outdoors or under glass in sufficient quantity a) To supply the whole population of the Estate, b) To stock the shop or shops fully by Whitsun 1978, and c) To have a small surplus to sell to other similar shops elsewhere.

Wheat. Plan now to *drill twenty acres* of winter wheat this

155

autumn. Never mind if 'experts' say it will not be fit for milling – it *will* be fit for milling. If we can produce fine bread here from wheat grown in *this* climate you can certainly grow good (soft) bread wheat in Devon. Start now (using Job Creation labour) building a small simple corn mill. If it has a waterwheel stuck on the side of it that really produces *some* of the power so much the better. It won't grind wheat any better than a diesel engine would but it will attract customers and get far more money out of the public than that at present useless waterwheel on the side of one of the textile factories. *Establish a bakery too.* Bake enough bread to supply everyone on the Estate, supply the shop or shops, and perhaps go a little further as well. Bake white bread as well as whole meal. People brought up to eat wrapped-pap take a little time to adapt to eating whole-meal bread baked from good English wheat – but there are a surprising number of people who *have* already made this adaptation!

Dairy. Sell one Friesian herd as soon as the price goes fairly high and use the money to buy forty jerseys and build a dairy. This could well be a cooperative enterprise too. Aim to produce luxury cheese of the Brie or Camembert type which will sell for a hell of a price right up-market, and also make (from the Friesian milk?) plenty of hard cheddar-type cheese for home consumption and also for sale. Put in a yoghourt-making plant, make butter (a loss-leader of course under the present subsidy arrangements), buttermilk, and unpasteurised whole milk. The marketing principle the same: first supply everyone on the Estate, then the shops and Cranks, then any surplus to other people.*

All skim and whey to the pigs of course.

Piggery. Buy now not more than thirty hardy gilts and run them out of doors in moveable arks and behind an electric fence. This piggery might be managed by an enthusiast but

---

*There is a splendid example of a cheese-making dairy of the right scale run by a member of 'The Ecologist' group, Wadebridge.

he must graze, or allow to root, his pigs under the direction of the Farm Manager, who will be expected to plant crops (jerusalem artichokes, fodder beet, etc.) for the pigs.

Sheep. Get the makings of a flock as soon as convenient, the breed to be chosen chiefly for the suitability of its wool. It should be the manager of the Textile Mill who chooses the breed. Meat will be an important, though secondary, object. The flock must be large enough to give a fair living to whoever is in charge of it (under the Farm Manager who will have the say in its movements).

Beef. Start rearing and fattening enough bull calves to supply Estate, and shops, with veal and beef, now.

Butchery. Establish one now for all classes of animals. Have also a bacon and ham curing room, smokery, etc. It would be necessary to find some real enthusiast to start this. Again - the highest quality products and right up-market. It is not a bit of good trying to compete with any product with the hoi-poloi. Don't try to make ordinary bangers. Send someone to Poland to learn to make the very finest continental-type smoked sausages.

Poultry on free range. Obviously should be the domain of an enthusiast, and moved about the farm under the direction of the Farm Manager. Enough for eggs and dressed poultry for all local needs and the shops.

Other enterprises that could follow quickly are *Brewery* (go to the Three Horseshoes in Bishops Castle, Salop, and have a look at theirs), *cider mill* (but obviously not until there were some apples - unless you could buy some cheap!). *Tannery, leather-works* - all such things on a workshop scale and run by skilled enthusiasts. It is not a bit of good starting such things on 'strictly commercial lines' and employing union labour.

Aim for the integration of all the other enterprises on the Estate with the Farms. After all - the Textile Mill is not exactly having a licence to print money now! Would it be such a great risk if it put some of its capacity over to processing and weaving local farm wool - and selling this, made up into garments, to a public which is becoming more and more keen

to buy country-made things and more and more fed up with
the over-finished and over-specialized? Supposing people knew
they could go to Dartington and actually see the sheep from
which their garment was shorn, and see the whole process right
through – would they not buy and (if the quality was right) pay
quite a lot over the odds? To compete on the world market
with every other textile mill in the world in run-of-the-mill
textiles must be a killing job. But the course I suggest would
not be competing with anybody. Dartington would be in a class
of its own. And what if a tailor in Totnes *did* start making suits
from the cloth woven from the wool of Dartington sheep? I for
one would have a suit off him and so, I guess, would a good
many other people.

The reason that will be given why none of the above
enterprises could pay is *the cost of labour.* Well if a lot of the
capital work could be done by Job Creation labour that knocks
a lot of the steam out of that argument, and, afterwards, the
running of these operations would not be done by ordinary
wage-earning union labour. They would mostly be run by
enthusiasts, who would always be looking for more ways of
making them pay and would be willing to work (as the kids on
my farm have been doing for *nothing* for the last eighteen
months) all the hours that they could stay awake. For they
would be working at what interests them for *themselves,* which
is the exact opposite of what most trade union members are
doing.

In setting up these enterprises a far more shoe-string approach should be used than is customary at Dartington. I
would undertake to knock up a very good flour mill, which
would grind all the flour that Dartington or its shops would
need and quite a lot over for selling on the apparently
insatiable 'whole-food organically-grown whole-meal flour'
market (at of course a good premium over the market that poor
Mr Rank has to sell his products on) for £10,000. And for that
probably be able to include a malting floor, kiln, oat-milling
stones, and a few other things like that and have some money

left over for working. And in all of these enterprises the impact on the *public* would be considered. No doubt an electrically fired bread oven would bake as good bread as a wood-fired one (fuelled on the large quantity of slash you must have to dispose of from felling in the forests) but the public would be intrigued and attracted by the wood-fired one – would come to look at it – and would buy the bread. They would end up by placing an order for weekly postal deliveries of Dartington Flour (Sam Mayall has an enormous mail-order business).

Meanwhile, all these activities would only be occupying a few small corners of the Farm lands. What would happen to the rest? It would go on being farmed much as it is now, but would slowly be pushed more in the direction of Organic Farming. One or two people like Sam Mayall should be retained as consultants. And gradually, over the years, more and more of Dartington lands would be taken over by labour-intensive activities such as we have been considering.

The Dartington Farms led the way into a new era in the nineteen twenties and thirties. They could lead the way into a new era now and I submit that should be their function.